Creating a Culture of Literacy:

A Guide for Middle and High School Principals

NATIONAL ASSOCIATION
of SECONDARY SCHOOL
PRINCIPALS

Reston, VA

1904 Association Drive
Reston, VA 20191-1537
800-253-7746
www.principals.org

Design by EEI Communications

Contents

Preface

Today, our nation is in danger. The danger I am describing here is pervasive and will attack the very core of our democracy. It comes from a lack of the most basic foundation of knowledge: the ability to read, write, and speak in a way that promotes further learning and advances ideas among diverse people. Without education, the wealthiest nations on earth can fall into poverty because—just like any organization—a nation's greatest asset is its people. As important as food and shelter are to human survival, education is to human development. Education makes it possible to think, dream, act, and build further knowledge. And there can be no education without literacy.

For too long, literacy has been considered the sole domain of the elementary grades, leaving behind too many older students who struggle through middle and high school. Our leaders are now more aware of the economic, social, and moral imperative of addressing the literacy needs of adolescents. President Bush proposed, and Congress passed, the Striving Readers Initiative, which begins to address this crisis at a federal level. Some states have also adopted an adolescent literacy initiative. The National Association of Secondary School Principals (NASSP) is proud to be part of this visionary movement. The 32,000 middle level and high school principals and assistant principals who are members of NASSP know all too well the effects poor literacy skills have on student achievement, future earning power, graduation rates, and school climate. For NASSP members and all other school leaders, we have developed this guide, which will give them tools to create and sustain a culture of literacy for all in their schools.

To lead this effort, we selected a person with whom readers would be able to identify. Melvina Phillips served as instructional administrator and principal of Discovery Middle School in Alabama. When the school first opened, student test scores ranked above the state and national levels on standardized tests; however, 25–30 percent of her students at each grade level were still reading below basic levels of achievement. To address this crisis, administration and staff worked collaboratively to implement and sustain a schoolwide plan. The results were dramatic:

- Students' core content scores on SAT 9 (social studies, science, language, and math) increased by an average of 10 percentile points over a four-year period.

- Alabama Direct Writing Scores improved because of the reading/writing connection across all content areas, with 27 percent of students scoring at Level 4 (top level) in 1996 and 79 percent of students scoring at Level 4 in 2002.

- Office referrals dropped from 682 to 127 due to active student engagement across the content areas.

Dr. Phillips also participated in The Alabama Reading Initiative: Literacy For All, a statewide literacy initiative that has become a model for other states. When she retired from the principalship, Dr. Phillips served as resident practitioner for adolescent literacy and professional development at NASSP and led hundreds of workshops for middle level and high school principals around the country. Her firsthand experience as a principal and her valuable knowledge of adolescent literacy add to the richness and effectiveness of the strategies outlined in this guide.

Gerald N. Tirozzi
Executive Director

Acknowledgments

We are deeply grateful to Carnegie Corporation of New York for funding the development of the guide. We would particularly like to thank Andrés Henríquez from the Corporation for his guidance and feedback throughout the development of this manuscript. We also wish to thank the Bill and Melinda Gates Foundation for providing a generous grant to allow for a wide distribution of this guide. Finally, this tool would not exist without the knowledge, experience, and writing ability of author Melvina Phillips, with the assistance of Patti Kinney, principal of Talent Middle School in southern Oregon and the 2003 MetLife/NASSP Middle Level Principal of the Year. Principal Mel Riddile and researcher Julie Meltzer, director of the Adolescent Literacy project at the Education Alliance at Brown University, provided valuable feedback and suggestions that improved the guide.

We also wish to thank the following principals and their staff members for sharing their school profiles:

- Terry Wolfson, Hopkins West Junior High School, Minnetonka, MN

- Mel Riddile, J.E.B. Stuart High School, Falls Church, VA

- Carol Hansen, Duncan Polytechnical High School, Fresno, CA

- Clara Sale-Davis, Freeport Intermediate School, Freeport, TX

- Tommy Ledbetter, Buckhorn High School., New Market, AL

1 Adolescent Literacy: What Do We Know?

Adolescent Literacy:
What Do We Know?   p. 1

Across the nation, there is increasing awareness of a major deficit in the literacy achievement of the country's secondary students. Studies such as the National Assessment of Educational Progress (NAEP) indicate that American students are reading and comprehending below expected levels. Eighth grade reading scores remain flat, and 12th grade scores have dropped significantly since 1992 (National Center for Education Statistics [NCES], 2001).

The National Center for Education Statistics (NCES) reports that there continues to be a significant achievement gap between certain demographic and ethnic groups on the NAEP reading assessment. Approximately 45–50 percent of black, Hispanic, and American Indian students score below the basic level on the NAEP, while less than 10 percent of whites and Asian/Pacific Islanders score less than basic. These disparities also hold true for students who are eligible for free and reduced-price school lunches compared to students from wealthier families (NCES, 2001). This inequity of achievement among student groups is begging for attention within the adolescent literacy issue.

Historically, direct literacy instruction has been supported up to the third grade. However, there is a glaring need for it to continue so students can not only read narrative text, but also learn specific strategies to derive meaning from expository and descriptive text. When literacy instruction stops early, how can middle and high school students learn the strategies to read increasingly difficult text and to comprehend more abstract ideas? If a "regular" student continues to need direct instruction to read and comprehend the text found in secondary textbooks, consider the tremendous need for instruction and intervention that struggling readers must require. And sadly, if students two to three grade levels behind their peers do not receive intensive literacy instruction, the results can be devastating because the struggling reader will not experience success within the content areas. Therefore, it becomes even more critical that secondary content area teachers better understand and teach specific literacy strategies to help students read and extract meaning from the written material used to teach the course content. Conclusions from the *RAND Reading Study Group* clearly support the need for continued literacy instruction at the middle and high school levels. (See Figure 1.1.)

Figure 1.1

RAND Reading Study Group Excerpts

The RAND (2002) study emphasized the following issues related to adolescent literacy:

- Comprehension is not increasing, but high school graduates are expected to read complex, technical material in order to be successful in the workforce

- Secondary students in the United States are scoring lower than students in other comparable nations. This is especially evident as secondary students deal with understanding discipline-specific content text

- There continues to be a gap in literacy performance between socioeconomic groups, ethnic groups, and **students with limited English proficiency**

- Secondary teachers are ill prepared to teach literacy strategies that are necessary for students' comprehension of content-specific text

- There is little empirical data to support some of the programs that are being implemented within many of the secondary schools.

Finding the Answers

Although there are no easy solutions for improving adolescent literacy, several key components appear to increase a student's opportunity for success. According to an International Reading Association (IRA, 1999) position statement, these components include, but are not limited to:

- Access to a variety of reading material

- Skill-building instruction that creates an interest in more complex reading material

- High-quality assessments that indicate weaknesses and strengths of students and the professional learning needs of teachers

- Highly skilled teachers who model and explicitly teach reading comprehension and study strategies across the content areas

- Reading specialists who apply explicit instructional strategies for the struggling reader.

In a recent report released by Carnegie Corporation of New York and the Alliance for Excellent Education, Biancarosa and Snow (2004) suggested 15 key elements that are indispensable to successful middle and high school literacy programs. The elements work together to impact the school's efforts in addressing the literacy needs of students from diverse backgrounds. The authors suggest a combination of instructional and infrastructure improvements that develop into a synergistic relationship to assist adolescent learners. (See Figure 1.2.)

In schools across the United States, adolescent students, regardless of their socio-economic status, are in critical need of intensive instruction to learn how to more successfully interact with and construct meaning from the texts they use daily. Caring, but misguided, teachers often ignore the *real* problem of struggling readers and simply provide notes or give students the facts on which they will be tested. Instead, teachers

Figure 1.2

Key Elements to Improve Middle and High School Adolescent Literacy Programs
(Biancarosa and Snow, 2004, p. 12)

Instructional Improvements

- Direct, explicit comprehension instruction
- Effective instructional principles embedded in content
- Motivation and self-directed learning
- Text-based collaborative learning
- Strategic tutoring
- Diverse texts
- Intensive writing
- A technology component
- Ongoing formative assessment of students

Infrastructure Improvements

- Extended time for literacy
- Professional development
- Ongoing summative assessment of students and programs
- Teacher teams
- Leadership
- A comprehensive and coordinated literacy program

need to tackle the root of the problem—these students do not read well enough to comprehend and derive meaning from the assigned text. Students who reach middle or high school and are still struggling to read for meaning should serve as a red flag to educators. We must move away from *this is the way we have always taught our subject* and instead commit to *what can I do to help my students read and comprehend the required reading.*

Statements released at an Alliance for Excellent Education (AEE, 2003) High School Summit are disturbing, if not downright frightening. In considering the merits of implementing a secondary literacy program for the students of our schools, the following statements should be examined and used as motivators to assure that **EVERY** student within the walls of U.S. schools is receiving literacy instruction across the content areas:

- There are 6 million students in grades 6 through 12 at risk of not graduating from high school or of graduating unprepared for success in college or a career

- Thirty percent of U.S. students are not graduating from high school

- Only 51 percent of African-American students and 52 percent of Hispanic students graduate from high school

- Seventy-five percent of students with literacy problems in the third grade will still experience literacy difficulties in the ninth grade

- The combined literacy score of 15-year-olds in the United States ranks 15th among developed countries

- Among 12th grade students, only 42 percent of whites, 16 percent of African Americans, and 22 percent of Hispanics scored at or above a proficient literacy level

- Approximately 25 percent of all high school students read below basic levels or three to four years below basic grade levels

- The graduation rate in urban schools is approximately 50 percent

- High school dropouts are about three times as likely as high school graduates to be welfare recipients
- Seventy-five percent of state prison inmates did not complete high school
- Every school day approximately 3,000 middle and high school students drop out of school.

Thoughts to Consider

The disheartening and alarming statistics of the research are clear. Literacy instruction must not stop as students enter middle school, but rather be a vital component of a student's educational experience from kindergarten to graduation. Poor literacy is not only an urban issue; it is found within every pocket of U.S. society. The time to rehash the issues and debate the problems of adolescent literacy has passed. There is a sense of urgency around finding solutions to this problem.

If secondary schools are to meet the academic instructional needs of the adolescent, there are several key elements that must be in place to fully implement an adolescent literacy program. (See Figure 1.3.) These essentials include (a) committed and supportive school leaders, (b) balanced formal and informal assessments that guide the learning of students and teachers, (c) ongoing, job-embedded, research-based professional development, (d) highly effective teachers in every content area that model and provide explicit instruction to improve comprehension, and (e) strategic and accelerated intervention.

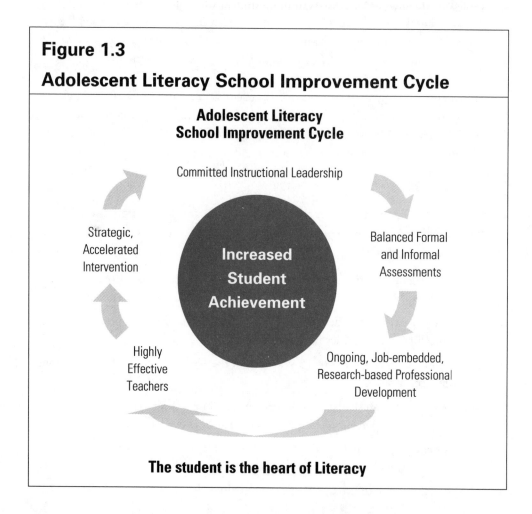

Figure 1.3

Adolescent Literacy School Improvement Cycle

Adolescent Literacy
School Improvement Cycle

Committed Instructional Leadership

Strategic, Accelerated Intervention

Balanced Formal and Informal Assessments

Increased Student Achievement

Highly Effective Teachers

Ongoing, Job-embedded, Research-based Professional Development

The student is the heart of Literacy

Although the task can appear to be overwhelming at first, a collaborative effort of administrators, faculty, and other key individuals can achieve a successful adolescent literacy program that will lead to student success. This book is designed to help a school use research on best literacy practices to create a well-defined intervention plan that will improve the literacy abilities of all students. By using the elements in Figure 1.2 as a foundation for implementing such a plan, schools will not only experience improved literacy in the present, but also impact the long-range academic success of their students by enhancing their chances for postsecondary education and future employability. It is a task that can no longer be ignored.

Guiding Questions for the Literacy Leader

Begin the journey to literacy improvement by addressing the following questions:

Adolescent Literacy: What Do We Know?

- How has my leadership supported literacy efforts at our school? Do *all* teachers view literacy as an integral part of the academic program? What structures and resources have I put in place to encourage literacy for all?

- What do our assessment scores reveal about our school's literacy practices? How is data being used to guide our school improvement plan? Do teachers have access to the data and use it to guide their instructional practices?

- What do I consider the key elements of our school's professional development plan? How do data and student literacy needs guide the development of the plan? Does our school structure support professional development by allowing time for professional conversations, for examining student work, and for learning new literacy strategies?

- Are content area teachers skilled at integrating literacy strategies into their daily lessons? What training have I provided for our teachers so they can be highly effective at delivering instruction in literacy in their content areas? Are our struggling students being taught by the most effective teachers?

- What support does our school provide for students who are below grade level in literacy? Does the schedule provide these students with additional, not pull-out, time to improve their skills? Do teachers use instructional strategies that support struggling students as they read textbooks and other content-area material?

Principal

2 Leadership: Unlocking the Door to Literacy

Strong leadership from both administrators and teachers is an essential building block in constructing a successful literacy program, but the role played by the principal is key to determining success or failure of the program. To have an effective program, the school leader must be involved in all aspects of planning and sustaining the program. Above all, this must include participation in professional development sessions so that he or she is fully aware of successful strategies needed to improve literacy across the curriculum. To be an effective literacy leader in the building, the principal must be viewed by the teachers as a role model of a reflective, life-long learner and have their respect as knowledgeable in the area of adolescent literacy.

To support the implementation of a schoolwide literacy program as an instructional leader, the principal must be highly visible throughout the school, regularly visiting classrooms to ensure that an emphasis on literacy is truly occurring. Participation in departmental and grade-level meetings allows the leader to be actively engaged with planning and evaluating the school's improvement efforts.

Formal classroom observations can result in more thorough implementation of research-based literacy strategies. Follow-up conferences can reinforce effective literacy instruction, promote the use of formal and informal assessment data to guide the literacy efforts, and provide opportunities to discuss further professional development needs.

For a literacy plan to succeed, the principal must also commit to developing a structure that supports the school's literacy efforts. For example, increased time for a language arts block that includes literacy and writing instruction is essential for improving literacy opportunities. Adequate or flexible scheduling also encourages opportunities to emphasize literacy throughout the content areas. It may also provide opportunities for adding a literacy elective for the struggling or striving adolescent learners. Common planning and/or team time allows teachers the opportunity to meet regularly to discuss instructional strategies that impact student achievement. The literacy leader is like a football coach or a conductor. Many elements must come together within the school to support literacy for every student. Individually, these elements may not seem difficult to achieve, but in isolation there is no success. Like a coach or conductor, the principal must skillfully pull the elements together in order to accomplish the ultimate goal—increased student achievement through improved literacy opportunities.

Leadership: Nine Action Steps for the Literacy Leader

1. Determine the school's capacity for literacy improvement.

Prior to initiating a schoolwide program to improve student literacy, the principal and staff should complete the Literacy Capacity Survey. (See Appendix 2.) This survey will help determine a school's strengths and needs for improvement in the area of literacy and spark conversations among staff about the need for such a program. Armed with information from the survey, the leader will be ready to begin the process that will ultimately lead to improved literacy practices and increased student achievement.

2. Develop a Literacy Leadership Team.

The first step a principal must take is to organize a Literacy Leadership Team (LLT) composed of administrators, content teachers, resource teachers, the literacy coach, and the media specialist. The counselor may also play an important role since he or she often meets entering students and may be first aware of individual needs. Representatives of this team should be active on the School Leadership Team, since literacy is central to the school's success.

The success of any literacy initiative depends upon having the support of the teaching staff from the beginning. As the concept of a secondary literacy initiative (or even literacy instruction) is often foreign to the traditional views of secondary curricula, teachers must be empowered and committed to understanding the problem and the need to develop an action plan for success. This best occurs when key teachers play a vital role in the LLT.

The literacy leader should carefully select highly motivated content-area teachers to serve on the LLT. The selected teachers should be highly skilled and deeply committed to improving the literacy opportunities for EVERY student. By serving on this team, teachers will influence the direction the school will travel as they make significant changes in the instructional program to support student learning through full integration of content literacy strategies. The literacy leader should keep in mind that the members selected for the LLT should have high energy and perseverance, as well as the ability to shake up the status quo and "make things happen" for the secondary student (National Association of Secondary School Principals [NASSP], 2004, p 23).

Members of the LLT analyze multiple forms of student, school, and teacher data to identify the academic learning needs of the students and the professional learning needs of the teachers. After gathering the data, team members need to identify and prioritize a list of students to be targeted for intervention or support and plan for the professional development of the staff.

Next, the LLT develops a list of needs and suggestions for improvement to share with the staff. This information should be used as a springboard for a professional conversation on school improvement with regard to literacy. Over time, through the leadership ability of the LLT, a collegial school culture committed to improved literacy for all will begin to evolve. The LLT assumes responsibility to guide the development and implementation of the Literacy Improvement Action Plan that uses assessment data to identify specific goals/objectives, persons responsible, activities/action, timeline, resources, and evaluation methods. It is important to remember that this plan should be inclusive of all activities necessary to support or expand literacy learning for all students. (See Appendix 3 for a Literacy Improvement Action Plan Template.)

The literacy leader's ability to pull all stakeholders together is paramount to the eventual success of the planned literacy improvement program. His or her primary role is to empower and build the capacity of the staff to meet the literacy learning needs of all students. This can best be accomplished by providing time and resources for the LLT to meet and plan. The LLT also needs access to the latest research on promising practices for adolescent literacy.

3. Create a collaborative environment that fosters sharing and learning.

The leader must establish a climate of collaboration and shared decisionmaking if the literacy plan is to succeed. He or she should encourage teacher leadership within the school by working with master teachers who can guide planning, modeling, organizing, and improving literacy instruction. It is also important to develop leadership skills in others and, when appropriate, give them authorization to make decisions and enact changes.

The literacy leader must provide opportunities for roundtable discussions related to problems teachers are facing as a result of their students' poor literacy skills. Through this discussion, teachers begin to realize they are facing some common problems with students within their respective classrooms. Problems of common interest may include students' inability to extract meaning of textbook literacy assignments or their inability to write coherently about a topic.

Literacy leaders encourage teacher support networks, or shared teaching, to discuss and observe best practices (ARI, 2003). If a collegial environment is to evolve, teachers need time to talk with one another about strategies that are working within their respective classrooms. When the building administrator encourages this sharing, teachers begin to rely more on one another to search for best practices that truly impact adolescent literacy. This type of collegiality also encourages the development of supportive relationships among teachers.

When discussing ways to improve teaching strategies, the collaborative principal must be an encourager and not a condemner; it is a fine line to walk because he or she should never be hesitant to suggest ways to improve the instructional process. Classroom observations by the principal should be supportive and result in the development of a plan to improve the instruction of literacy skills within the content area. The principal's knowledge base must be extensive enough to provide suggestions for improvement when the classroom teacher is seeking help.

Collaborative leaders celebrate success. Highlight in the weekly bulletin or e-mail the best strategies observed. Provide opportunities during faculty meetings to watch a brief video of a content-area teacher successfully using a specific literacy strategy. Encourage teachers to share their stories of success with one another.

4. Develop a schoolwide organizational model that supports extended time for literacy instruction.

The literacy leader needs to carefully examine the school's structure to determine if sufficient time is available for literacy instruction. If not, he or she needs to take on the challenge of designing a structure that allows for it. An extended period of time (90 to 100 minutes) for language arts within a block or flexible schedule is essential to meet the challenges of improved literacy. With the additional time provided, teachers can increase direct instruction in reading and writing, allow more time for students to read and connect with the material, and implement integrated learning tasks. Adequate scheduling should also include opportunities for teachers to work in collaborative teams to plan and assess teaching strategies based on student achievement data.

Students who are three to four years behind need intensive intervention. The schedule must be designed to give them the opportunity to receive support from a highly skilled literacy specialist who can diagnose and provide a prescriptive literacy intervention program. For many schools, this means allocating time during the day for necessary literacy electives.

Flexible or block schedules require teachers to make a shift in their instructional practices. The literacy leader must provide professional development opportunities in order for this to occur. Content teachers must analyze their lessons to determine if they are spending too much time in lecturing and note taking instead of using strategies to reinforce understanding of the textbook. The leader must visit classrooms to analyze class activities and support the use of appropriate literacy strategies in the content areas. If students are to improve literacy, then teachers must spend time teaching with strategies that support reading and comprehension.

---

5. Analyze assessment data to determine specific learning needs of students.

Standardized tests can serve as a baseline to determine which students are reading below grade level. However, multiple forms of assessment must be properly used and interpreted to fully understand student and teacher strengths and weaknesses. Class grades, teacher anecdotal records, and informal and formal assessments provide invaluable information if used properly to identify specific deficiencies in literacy.

Every teacher should know and understand what the data reveal about the literacy abilities of each student within his or her classroom. Once abilities are determined, classroom teachers should work closely with the literacy coach or special education teacher to develop an action plan to address the specific learning needs of the students within their classes.

It is important to remember that standardized tests are designed to identify where students fall in relation to other students' achievement levels. Because it is impossible to help students if their deficiencies are not properly identified, students must be assessed using a test intended to identify detailed information about the students' literacy levels—strengths and deficits. Data on each individual child should be kept in a secure location but should be readily accessible so that individual or groups of teachers can use the data as they plan an instructional program for the student/s.

Determining how to use the data is critical to making a difference for students. If assessment data are not used to improve learning, then it becomes just another assessment to set on the shelf. Instructional leaders, along with faculty, must fully understand the data and how to use the analyses to develop a school improvement plan. The results of the analyses should guide both the intervention plan for students and the professional development plan for teachers.

6. Develop a schoolwide plan to address the professional development needs of teachers.

The LLT should use student assessment results, teacher assessments, and surveys to determine the staff's professional development needs. Most secondary teachers are not prepared to teach literacy strategies within the content area; therefore, the initial staff development for most schools should focus on strategies that improve comprehension, strengthen the reading/writing connection, and enhance content-area literacy instruction.

When planning for the initial staffwide professional development, half-day sessions with master teachers, literacy practitioners, and other literacy resource professionals are the ideal. These are best held during the in-service week before school begins or on an in-service day during the year. However, scheduling time for these sessions generally requires district approval and should be done prior to the development of the next school year's calendar.

The administrator's job is to not only assure that the initial professional development takes place, but also to plan with teachers for job-embedded, research-based professional development that continues throughout the year. The principal's position becomes critical to this process because he or she must find the necessary time for this type of professional development.

Finding time for job-embedded professional development is often a balancing act between providing students with high-quality teaching during the day and providing teachers time for professional growth. As alternatives to using substitutes, schools can consider taking advantage of planned in-service days, delayed starts or early releases, team planning time, before school breakfasts, or after school discussion groups. With considerable preplanning, the lunch block may provide time for teacher professional book studies, student support teams, departmental meetings, grade level teams, and mentor/mentee collaboration time. If it is possible to build a cadre of parent para-professionals willing and able to help cover teacher duties, then a luncheon professional development period can become reality.

7. Create a realistic budget for literacy needs.

If a secondary school literacy initiative is to be successful, increased funding must be available to support the purchase of necessary materials such as books for the media center, classroom sets of novels and/or nonfiction books, test protocols, software, etc. Further costs come in the form of professional development and possibly additional teaching or support staff.

The first step the LLT should take is to prioritize the needs of the school and determine what costs are essential to the immediate implementation of the program and what may be purchased in following years. This prioritized list will serve as a road map for the principal as he or she determines possible funding sources to meet the needs.

The principal must closely examine the school's budget to determine spending trends and look for monies that can be shifted to support literacy efforts. For example, if a particular department has not used its entire budget for the last several years, the difference between the budgeted amount and the actual expenses could be shifted to support literacy efforts. This can become a collaborative effort if the school has built a culture that supports improved literacy efforts for all; the principal can challenge teachers or departments to determine how much from their budget could be used in their effort to improve their student's literacy achievement.

Title funds from the federal government are another funding source that can support a school's literacy plan. If the school has a large portion of English language learners, Title III monies can be used to give literacy support to this population. Title II funds can be used to improve literacy knowledge through appropriate staff development. It is critical that the principal works with the district administrator who oversees these funds and coordinates with the school's professional development committee to develop a plan to utilize this funding. To be eligible for these federal dollars, activities must be based on assessment data that indicate the learning needs of professional staff.

Business partnerships are another major source of funding. Business leaders are interested in improving the overall literacy of the nation's graduates, and they are usually eager to support efforts that will improve student literacy, writing, and speaking. The principal's job is to seek sources of corporate funding and to develop the relationships that will assure that the funding will flow to the local school. Parent groups may also be willing to raise money to support student literacy efforts, and many businesses offer programs that give schools a percentage of designated purchases made at their stores.

Private grants are also a valuable source of funding to support literacy programs. The amounts may range from small to large, and the principal must determine how the funding can be best used to support the planned local literacy program. Grant writing should be a schoolwide effort, with both teachers and administrators involved in writing the grants.

There are also opportunities to pilot programs for publishing, testing, and software companies. This can be an excellent resource if the product fits into the school literacy plan, and the company will allow the school to keep the product after piloting. The principal and literacy committee must be very careful to agree to pilot only programs that are research-based and are fully understood by the staff. *Caution:* The focus is to improve literacy at the school, not just adopt a program, so be careful with this option.

---

8. Develop a broad understanding of literacy strategies that work in the content-area classes.

While the principal may not be highly proficient in the delivery of literacy strategies in all content areas, as an instructional leader, he or she should be familiar with proven literacy strategies and be able to converse with content teachers about strategies that help students to activate prior knowledge, develop metacognition, and expand thinking and understanding of text.

Literacy leaders should regularly be in classrooms to observe implementation of explicit literacy strategies within content classes. This practice provides principals with critical knowledge related to student learning, as well as insight into the professional development needs of teachers. Principals are ultimately accountable for student learning, and one of the best strategies for guaranteeing that students meet tough academic standards is to assure that all teachers are skillfully integrating literacy strategies into daily instruction.

9. Demonstrate your commitment to the literacy program.

To motivate staff, the principal needs to promote a team-based approach and remain actively engaged in the literacy initiative. This process begins with attending professional development sessions and not just sending a teacher or a team to learn about literacy instruction. When staff members see that the principal is committed to learning new literacy strategies, they begin to view the principal as truly resolute when it comes to improving literacy instruction.

And Remember...

- Success begins with the principal. The staff will look to their building leader to determine his or her support for a literacy program. A lack of commitment by either words or actions will kill the program before it begins.

- Time to talk is critical if teachers are to share their experiences with one another and discuss instructional strategies that work. Find that time for them.

- The schedule should not drive school programs. While constraints of personnel and course offerings can make a schedule seem inflexible, do not give up—think creatively, talk with colleagues, research organizational models. You will not find a perfect model that will solve all the scheduling needs for your building, but you may be able to use ideas from several sources to find one that works best for your school.

- Remember, prospective funders can only say "no." Be bold in your efforts to seek additional funding sources to support your literacy efforts. Ask politely, giving a clear rationale. If they say "no," thank them for their time and willingness to listen. You never know when a "no" will turn into a "yes" at some future time.

Leadership:
Unlocking the Door to Literacy

Learn More About It:
What the Experts and Research Say About Leadership

Leadership plays a pivotal role in a secondary school's ability to establish a successful literacy program. A study released by the Wallace Foundation (Leithwood, Anderson, and Wahlstrom, 2004) found that school leadership is "second only to teaching among school-related factors in its impact on student learning," and this certainly holds true for the implementation of a schoolwide literacy plan. While the creation and implementation of such a plan must be a collaborative effort among teachers and administrators, it is the building principal's role as a literacy leader that has the greatest impact on the plan's outcome.

Instructional leaders must be committed to improving classroom instruction, professional learning, student assessment and achievement, and the use of collegial classroom observations to support and improve reflective teaching (Schon, 1988). An effective principal makes the difference by improving literacy opportunities for all students, by providing professional learning opportunities for teachers, and by staying actively involved in the development of the school's improvement plan.

In 2001, several nationally recognized literacy researchers met with representatives of the Children's Literacy Network to discuss steps that literacy administrators should follow in order to assure successful literacy opportunities for students. The recommendations

CHAPTER 2: LEADERSHIP: UNLOCKING THE DOOR TO LITERACY   13 that follow placed the strongest emphasis on the principal's need to have a clear under-standing of the best practices with regard to adolescent literacy.

- Principals need to have a broad grasp of what it takes to understand, and change if necessary, the school culture needed to impact literacy. It is important to create an atmosphere of collegiality so that teachers can work and learn from one another.

- Principals should research the work of respected practitioners in order to gain an understanding of best practices related to improving literacy.

- Principals should *read, read, read*. Literacy material should include professional literature related to adolescent literacy. Principals should also read books for and about adolescent readers so that they gain a better grasp of the literature.

- Principals should develop a thorough understanding of the best and most current instructional models. If the collegial environment has been created, the principal can easily open the discussion about successful instructional models and how to best implement the plan into practice.

- Principals need to have a thorough understanding of national, state, and local curriculum standards and know if their teachers have the ability to successfully deliver the content.

- Principals should organize and wisely use facilities and time to create an environ-ment that encourages increased emphasis on literacy.

- Principals need to understand the data that are provided by multiple assessments and how to use this information to improve student and teacher learning.

- Principals need to explore funding sources, scheduling, and creative ways to meet the specific learning requirements of the struggling reader.

- Principals should be aware of successful models and organizations that are devoted to finding what works best. It is important to have an ally to turn to when researching or trying to implement a literacy program that works (Children's Literacy Network, 2001).

The principal must also work to develop a flexible organizational structure that allows time for literacy instruction. As far back as 1984, Goodlad identified that sec-ondary students actively read for only 2 percent of their class time (cited in Frey, M., Zipperer, M., Worley, M., Sisson, M., & Said, R., 2002). Further research indicates that students' comprehension, fluency, and vocabulary increase if the student has more time to read (California Dept. of Education, 1996; Pearson et al., 1992; Anderson, R., Wilson, P., & Fielding, L., 1988).

Hopkins West Junior High School

The Journey Begins

Hopkins West Junior High, located outside of Minneapolis, MN, is a school where a culture of literacy exists due to the visionary leadership of Principal Terry Wolfson. She and a core group of teachers first explored strategies to improve their students' literacy skills at the summer 2000 Scholastic Literacy Leadership Institute (jointly sponsored by Scholastic and NASSP). This initial foray into improving the literacy skills of their students quickly evolved into a literacy-infused school culture. While the students are the direct beneficiaries of this change, Ms. Wolfson quickly identifies the professional learning opportunities for teachers as another key benefit. The total focus on literacy that permeates the building is one of high achievement for both teachers and students.

The journey began when the school's traditionally high test scores were first disaggregated in 1999. Although the pass rate on the Minnesota Minimum Basic Standards Test was 90 percent, data indicated a wide achievement gap existed for students of color and poverty. This data sparked a conversation among the leadership team to identify strategies for improving the reading ability of lower-achieving students. The reading department chair quickly expressed the idea that enhanced literacy opportunities should not be for a chosen few, but rather be directed at benefiting all students.

The seventh grade team provided the initial leadership to improve literacy by attending the Literacy Leadership Institute along with Wolfson. In addition to learning new strategies at the conference, the team had time to strategically plan together. They returned to Hopkins realizing if literacy for all was to be achieved, then all teachers must learn to integrate literacy strategies into their daily instruction. With this goal in mind, the administration and staff began to plot the areas of improvement for the literacy journey.

Organizing for a New Focus

The Literacy Leadership Institute provided the attendees with the motivational spark to return to Hopkins with a message to share with the remainder of the staff. The original seventh grade team began a pilot program in their classrooms to integrate literacy across content areas. But the school's highly motivated staff quickly picked up the enthusiasm of this team and began to explore schoolwide options that would focus on adolescent literacy.

The first priority of the literacy planning team was to legitimize the goal of literacy for all; therefore, literacy became a primary *tactic* (goal) of the school improvement plan. Originally, the plan included four tactics: diversity, communication, use of time, and literacy. After careful planning and evaluation, the team refined the school's *tactics* to two critical areas—literacy and equity. When this occurred, all fiscal and human resources were directed at developing a school culture that would support literacy and equity for all.

The planning team first evaluated the school's schedule to identify what changes were needed to support teacher planning and instruction. Their findings resulted in revising the existing eight-periods-per-day schedule into an alternating-day block schedule that would allow for extended instructional time. This change allowed the

Profile

Hopkins West Junior High School

3830 Baker Road Minnetonka, MN 55305

Principal: Terry Wolfson

- *950 students*
- *18 percent minority (83 percent white, 8 percent black, 7 percent Hispanic, 2 percent Asian/other)*
- *13 percent free and reduced-price meals*
- *Grades: 7–9*
- *Recognitions: NASSP Highly Successful Middle Level School*

integration of literacy into daily content instruction, thus creating an environment that was supportive of student literacy, learning, and achievement.

Benefits of the improved schedule also included opportunities for teacher collaboration and planning. A block of common planning time permitted teachers to work as a team to evaluate student achievement and work samples, as well as make necessary adjustments to instruction as they planned lessons together. Collaborative planning encouraged the selection of appropriate literacy strategies and best instructional practices to support learning within each team. Perhaps the greatest value of team collaboration was the opportunity for professional conversations and growth that added to their knowledge base of literacy strategies.

Assessment and Professional Development to Support the Literacy Tactic

Ms. Wolfson is quick to stress the importance of a highly effective teaching staff. As she interviews perspective teachers, she searches for ones who will be successful content literacy teachers. Nevertheless, there still remained a critical need for continuing professional development to support literacy instruction. Since very few content teachers possessed the skills to integrate literacy strategies into their daily lessons, the original literacy planning team identified professional development as a cornerstone for their goal of achieving literacy for all. Understanding assessment was also a key element of the professional development required to support student achievement.

Several practices are in place at Hopkins to support data-driven professional development. The school assessment team, consisting of the administration and four teachers, attend an annual summer data retreat and completely focus on the assessment data. With support from district assessment experts, the team analyzes individual student data and determines instructional needs. This activity puts the focus on student needs, as well as revealing additional professional development required to support student learning objectives.

There are several practices in place to support literacy professional development. Although Hopkins does not have a literacy coach, there are highly effective teacher-leaders on the staff who coach and support the learning of literacy instructional practices and strategies. Within the planning block, teachers model literacy strategies for one another and hold professional conversations regarding literacy issues. However, Wolfson indicates coaching is still not at the level desired and believes a literacy coach would be an added benefit for Hopkins' literacy efforts. Another structure in place to support literacy professional development includes seven late start days built into the school's calendar.

Instruction Supports Literacy Culture

A Literacy Walk through the school reveals a culture of literacy that permeates the hallways and classrooms. Word walls supporting vocabulary development are found throughout the building. Classrooms contain their own libraries used to support literacy and learning. Teachers effectively using David Hyerls's *Thinking Maps Framework* actively engage students in thinking critically about text. Science teachers provide a picture of the literacy integration with their creative use of picture books such as *Everyone Poops*. This serves as a prereading anticipatory activity to hook students' interest in learning more about the expository topic of the body's excretory system. In each classroom there is evidence of strategic teaching to help students make connections using pre, during, and post literacy strategies. The Scope and Sequence of Literacy Skills, developed by teachers, includes pre, during, and post literacy instructional strategies. Classroom instruction focuses on literacy strategies for all students.

Intervention to Support Students with Most Critical Literacy Needs

Armed with data, the staff takes a proactive approach to meeting students' literacy requirements. One successful strategy has been the *Zoom* transition program for incoming seventh grade students. Students identified as candidates for additional support attend *Zoom,* a four-week, literacy-rich, interrelationship-building session. From the 30 students who attend this session, approximately 15 are selected for an intensive reading and writing intervention class. The class meets for 90 minutes per day, and two teachers loop with the students through eighth grade. Ms. Wolfson indicated the original program has been so successful that they now offer eighth and ninth grade *Zoom* experiences. Another vital component of the Hopkins' reading program is Scholastic's READ 180. Even with these effective approaches in place, the most critical ingredient for success continues to be placement of the very best teachers with students requiring the most intensive intervention.

The Journey Continues

The literacy efforts at Hopkins are paying off. While the school's population continues to become more diverse, students scored the best yet on statewide assessments given in spring 2004. But the professional staff at Hopkins understands they cannot rest on their laurels. Careful analyses of data, ongoing professional development, and nurturing the culture to support literacy is an ever-changing, continuous process. The stage is set for continued success, and students, teachers, and administrators will continue to persist with the mission of literacy for all.

School Profile 1:
Hopkins West Junior High School

Standardized test scores may also provide general baseline data on individual students. If a student scored below the 50th percentile in a future...

3 Putting Assessment in the Driver's Seat

The goal of a school's assessment efforts should be to provide a clear picture of student strengths and weaknesses, teacher professional development needs, and the school's capacity to support a school literacy program. To meet this goal, the school will need to develop a balanced assessment program that uses both formal and informal measures of achievement in gathering data to determine the success of the program.

Formal data, such as standardized test scores, can provide a baseline for evaluating school literacy achievement and can be used to track group progress from year to year. Standardized test scores may also provide general baseline data on individual student, i.e., a student scoring below the 50th percentile or in stanines 1–4 is likely to have reading difficulties. However, the major limitation of standardized test scores is if the information garnered does not provide specific data leading to prescriptive activities that will improve student reading and comprehension.

To adequately identify areas of instructional focus, more specific literacy tests should be used. Many such tests are available; choose one that is valid, reliable, provides explicit information related to literacy skills, and can be used for pre and post testing. Whatever the choice, be consistent and do not change tests from year to year. (See Appendix 4 for a list of assessment instruments appropriate for secondary students.)

Informal assessments come in many forms, and their value cannot be dismissed from the total assessment plan. Teacher anecdotal records, informal assessments, student reflective journals, student strategy–use records, portfolios, class grades, and student surveys provide invaluable information that paints a more thorough picture of the individual student's literacy deficiencies and strengths.

Assessment should be both formative and summative. Data that are collected but not evaluated during and after the implementation of a program, strategy, or literacy improvement plan become a meaningless collection of numbers. Timelines for conducting and analyzing formative and summative assessments provide a framework that keeps everyone on target so that assessment becomes a tool for improvement. The principal should work with the leadership team and faculty to schedule data- or progress-monitoring meetings throughout the school year.

If assessment of practice is not ongoing, then valuable time can be wasted in the effort to improve student literacy. As teachers implement new instructional literacy strategies, formative assessments can determine if the practice is successful. Teachers may also want to conduct action research projects to evaluate how these new practices impact student learning.

Data from summative evaluations of the literacy program enable the staff and administrator to make revisions to the literacy action plan if needed. Summative data to consider are posttests that provide a standard score for each student's literacy progress and fully assess the student's literacy strengths and weaknesses. Results of summative teacher evaluations and observations help the administrator and teacher determine needs for further professional development. Formative and summative evaluations also help to identify master teachers who may serve as mentors or models for other teachers trying to improve classroom delivery of literacy instruction.

> *It is the action around assessment—the discussion, meetings, revisions, arguments, and opportunities to continually create new directions for teaching, learning, curriculum, and assessment— that ultimately have consequences. The "things" of assessment are essentially useful as dynamic supports for reflection and action, rather than as static products with value in and of themselves.*
>
> (Darling-Hammond, Ancess, and Falk 1995, p. 18)

Assessment: Seven Action Steps for the Literacy Leader

1. Become an assessment-savvy leader.

The principal's role is critical to the assessment process. It is not a job for the weak-spirited because using data to drive instruction often requires making significant changes in curricula, scheduling, and staff. In order to accomplish this, principals should have a comprehensive knowledge of how to collect, analyze, and interpret data. As the primary leader of the school, the principal's initiative and focus on using data to guide school improvement efforts will profoundly impact how the staff views the importance of assessment data. If the principal has established a climate of collaboration and shared decision making at the school, the staff and community will more easily accept decisions brought about by an analysis of the data.

Working with the LLT and staff, a savvy leader will analyze test data to identify strengths and weaknesses of the literacy instructional program. Test scores should be analyzed for trends. Are students' scores consistently low in one skill area? Which skill areas are identified as areas of strength? Are there identifiable trends found in grade levels or departmental teams? What are the strengths and weaknesses of the instructional program?

Trends in student achievement can be wisely interpreted only if several years of data are collected. Developing a system to track student achievement through multiple years of grades and standardized test scores is invaluable for the LLT. Spreadsheets are especially helpful as they allow the team to develop graphs and charts that document progress and trends. (See Appendix 5 for a five-year data collecting template.)

Once the assessment data have been recorded and analyzed, the principal, along with the LLT, should use the results to evaluate the literacy proficiency of students, needs for teacher professional development, and the quality of the overall instructional program. This evaluation will help the leadership team to refine the school literacy program.

2. Use data from assessments wisely and in a balanced fashion.

With increased emphasis on accountability and high-stakes tests, there is a danger of allowing one test to dictate our instructional programs. These tests are important and schools should assure that the curricula are closely aligned with local, state, and national standards. However, no one assessment can present a true picture of a student's achievement level or predict the success or failure of the school. Wise leaders will work with the staff to develop a balanced assessment program to guide the instructional program.

To improve individual literacy ability, and ultimately the school literacy level, there must be an assessment tool that identifies specific literacy strengths and weaknesses. An effective assessment tool will provide a standard score, grade equivalent, and specific identification of literacy weaknesses and strengths. But to fully understand the literacy needs of the student, educators must look at other assessments to complete the picture. These include informal methods such as observations, checklists, anecdotal records, literacy logs or portfolios, and informal literacy inventories. (A more thorough explanation of these techniques appears later in this chapter under "What the Experts and Research Say.")

Secondary teachers are struggling to understand their role in the teaching of literacy, so it is important to start the process by introducing ways to observe adolescents' literacy skills and to derive meaning from the observations. To help prepare the staff for this task, it is important to provide training so they understand and use:

- Reading and writing strategies employed by proficient readers

- Strategies for observing and recording students' interests and attitudes related to literacy

- Techniques for analyzing and understanding what the data reveal.

3. Establish a school culture that utilizes data to guide a literacy program designed to meet the needs of ALL learners, both students and teachers.

Effective school administrators develop a collaborative, reflective school culture. In creating a schoolwide literacy program, it is important to capitalize on that culture as the staff work together to analyze data and develop an action plan to address the learning needs of students and teachers. For a program to be effective, every staff member should be engaged in analyzing, evaluating, and discussing student work as a means of increasing student achievement.

The principal will also need to foster collaboration as the staff work together to develop a schoolwide literacy program that addresses the literacy needs of the students. This endeavor begins with LLT analyzing both formal and informal student data. The analysis should identify strengths and weaknesses of the school literacy program (or the lack of one). Once the analysis is complete, the data should be reported back to the staff and then used to develop a literacy intervention plan (Chapter 6 for more).

It is imperative that the staff play a role in developing a professional learning program that addresses their specific literacy needs. Questions to be considered include the following: Do the teachers have the knowledge base and expertise to provide instruction with literacy strategies within the content area? If not, what professional development does the data indicate is needed by the staff? What information do the teachers need in order to support a secondary literacy program? The answers to these questions will provide a framework for the development and implementation of a comprehensive professional development program. Chapter 4 treats this topic in greater depth.

4. Implement regular data- and progress-monitoring meetings.

Periodic progress-monitoring meetings about student achievement are a significant tool for formative assessment (ARI, 2003). These meetings may be held monthly or at the end of each grading period. The team evaluating current data is normally composed of the literacy coach, classroom teachers, the counselor, and the administrator.

The purpose of the meeting is to track student progress after the initial collection of data. The participants bring class work samples and discuss literacy strategies used in content classes that have improved student performance. There should also be informal literacy assessment data to indicate students' mastery of literacy skills and areas for focus.

After evaluating current data, a progress-monitoring team should determine what adjustments are needed in the Student's Individual Literacy Improvement Plan. Key questions to consider when developing/revising the student plans include the following:

What literacy strategies should content-area teachers use? Content area teachers should strategically plan the inclusion of pre, during, and post literacy strategies during their daily instruction. They should document strategies used in lesson plans and evaluate student progress and success with strategies. The progress-monitoring session provides an opportunity to evaluate the success of strategy integration. The ultimate indicator is student achievement and how students are succeeding due to the use of specific literacy strategies. If students are not achieving success, additional strategies may be designed and implemented. The progress-monitoring team should work together to develop strategies that provide a strategic and consistent approach to helping students learn essential literacy strategies.

What additional interventions are needed to guide the student toward success? The literacy coach/specialist may need to provide one-on-one skill instruction or determine what other intensive intervention strategies may be employed to encourage student success. The progress-monitoring sessions should provide valuable insight into the student's progress and the current instructional program. The information garnered is a valuable tool to make adjustments as required. (Appendix 6 provides an example of an Individual Progress Monitoring Template.)

5. Use data to bring teachers to a full awareness of student achievement levels to meet the individual needs of *all* learners within *all* classes.

The nation's teachers are working hard but not always achieving the results that we desire. Students in the upper echelon of the socioeconomic level are achieving higher than the students prior to this generation, but the question and dilemma remains: What are we to do with the students not achieving at proficient levels, and how do we address this achievement gap?

More and more schools are comprised of diverse student populations, bringing their diverse literacy needs into the classroom. Second language learners have multiplied, and classes are comprised of students from across many socioeconomic backgrounds. Therefore, delivery of instruction needs to be directed at meeting the multiple learning styles and needs of today's students. To fully understand diverse student populations within the school, it is vital to disaggregate data (see Appendix 7).

To address this issue, teachers must have access to formal and informal data on each student they serve in the classroom. When all teachers have the opportunity to gain an understanding of their students' achievement strengths and weaknesses, instruction will improve. This understanding does not come with a cursory look at assessment data, but rather an in-depth analysis of all existing data that paints a picture of a need for change and improvement. At this point, it is crucial that the principal provide teachers with access to specialists who can impart best strategies to improve the instructional delivery for each student.

At departmental or team meetings, teachers should analyze assessments to learn what curriculum and/or instructional practices need changing. In student support teams, they should carefully analyze student work and assessments to evaluate student achievement as well as the effectiveness of their own instructional practices at meeting the needs of EVERY student. This is a critical step in the assessment process, because teachers learn so much by discussing and planning for improvement together. It again calls upon the principal's skill to build a spirit of collaboration because improving literacy begins with the analysis of data, building of trust, and learning from one another.

6. Conduct a weekly Literacy Walk to assess implementation of literacy strategies.

A Literacy Walk provides insight related to the successful implementation of literacy strategies into the day-to-day instructional program. The LLT should regularly conduct a walk-through of content classes to collect informal assessment data on instructional strategies and student engagement.

A Literacy Walk should not be a threatening device, but a tool that encourages collaborative conversations aimed at increasing a teacher's knowledge and skill at delivering literacy instruction. To alleviate teacher concerns, the purpose of this informal assessment/learning format must be thoroughly understood before implementation. It is not a formal teacher observation, but simply a tool to spark discussions and reinforce the literacy emphasis within the school. This tool has been quite successful in schools that participate in the ARI. The strategy also provides effective identification of professional development needs. Chapter 4 treats the Literacy Walk in greater depth.

7. Use outside experts to guide the use of appropriate assessment tools for your school.

Educators often have only a minimal knowledge of how to choose and interpret the *best* type of assessments needed to implement an effective adolescent literacy program. Calling upon experts in the area of assessment to work with the school can provide prescriptive suggestions for instructional change as well as ways to work with adolescent learners to increase literacy achievement.

Consultants from testing organizations can provide information about informal assessments, standardized assessments, surveys, and other tools that may be appropriate for your individual school community. Collaborating with a testing company will provide specifics about assessment tools that can be tailored to the school's situation. A company representative may permit your staff to pilot the use of a test protocol. Additionally, the company may work with you to score large administrations of tests. Although you do not want to commit to one test, testing companies can be a valuable resource to your school through their advice and services.

Professors and graduate students from local universities may be willing to provide technical assistance as you evaluate assessment results. They may help analyze the results of evaluations and work with staff to develop an action plan for improvement. By working on specific instructional strategies to improve literacy learning, their assistance may also provide additional professional development opportunities for the staff. Graduate students can often provide additional help with the administration and the follow-up scoring of individual literacy assessments. Further assistance may come in the guise of tutoring of students with identified literacy weaknesses.

Other help may be available from psychometricians from the local school district or the state department of education. These individuals are experts in the area of testing and can assist you and your staff with the selection of assessment tools and interpretation of the results. They can often help you identify trends and understand your scores in relation to other schools with similar demographics.

And Remember...

- The informal assessments and expert observations done by staff members play a vital role in understanding the needs of your students and your staff.

- Always bear in mind that the steps you take to implement an action plan must be based on the assessment data.

- The most important consideration for the school administrator and staff when evaluating the school literacy assessment program: Is the assessment program balanced and does it consist of both formal and informal assessments? Both formal and informal assessments should be the order of the day. One test should never guide all improvement efforts.

- It is the collaborative planning for assessment and the ongoing analysis of the data that result in improved instruction and increased student achievement.

- And above all, do not forget that the ultimate success of the students is the driving purpose of assessment.

Learn More About It:
What the Experts and Research Say About Assessment

According to Grant Wiggins (1997), assessment and learning cannot be separated when planning a secondary literacy program. Therefore, both formal and informal assessments must be consistently utilized and analyzed if they are to play a significant role in improving the literacy program of a school. Examples of each appear below in Figure 3.1.

To adequately identify areas of instructional focus, a standardized literacy test such as the ones listed on the next page should be used. Many such tests exist; the critical point is to find a test that is valid, reliable, and provides valuable insight into the student's literacy ability and areas for improvement. The key to the selection of an assessment instrument is that the test provides a standard score and other explicit information related to literacy skills.

The informal assessments described in the following section can be used at the middle and high school levels. Although many of these assessments are associated with elementary readers, they are still appropriate for use as an informal assessment instrument at the secondary level.

Figure 3.1

Informal and Formal Assessment Instruments

Informal Assessments	Formal Assessments
■ Content Area Literacy Assessments	■ Stanford Achievement Test
■ Teacher Observations	■ California Achievement Test
■ Qualitative Reading Inventory III	■ Group Reading Assessment and Diagnostic Evaluation (GRADE)
■ Informal Literacy Inventories	■ Test of Reading Comprehension (TORC-3)
☐ Scholastic	■ Gray Oral Reading Tests-Diagnostic (GORT-D)
☐ Teacher Developed	■ Stanford Diagnostic Reading Test 4
• Diagnostic Interview	■ Woodcock-Johnson Reading Mastery
• Preparation for Reading	
• Silent Reading	
• Oral Reading	
• Retelling	
■ Miscue Analysis	
■ Burns/Roe Informal Reading Inventory	
■ Retellings	
■ Cloze Procedure	
■ Student Interest and Attitude Surveys	
■ Other Important Data	
☐ Report Grades	
☐ Student Demographic Data	
☐ Promotion/Retention Data	
☐ Disciplinary Records	
☐ Attendance Data	

Putting Assessment in the Driver's Seat

Informal Assessments

Class observation. Secondary readers can often pronounce words accurately, but they cannot derive meaning from the text. Close observation by the teacher can help identify specifics of the literacy difficulty. When using this type of observation, the teacher can immediately identify if a student is struggling with word identification skills or fluency. Other data derived from close observation may require more in-depth knowledge of the literacy process. Questions to be answered from a close observation of the student are:

■ Does the student understand the meaning of what is read?

■ What literacy strategies does the student use to help extract meaning from the text?

■ Does the student give up when he or she encounters new words or difficult passages?

Checklists and observation guides. By using checklists and observation guides, the teacher can identify the students' use of strategies, progress, and literacy interests. When observation guides are used several times during the school year, patterns begin to materialize that provide teachers with information related to student progress. Figure 3.2 provides an example of a checklist/observation guide.

Figure 3.2

Literacy Checklist and Observation Guide Example

Student Name: _____

☐ Uses context clues to understand text.

☐ Selects graphic organizers to use during reading.

☐ Rereads when meaning is unclear.

☐ Uses text structure to support understanding.

Comments/Observations:_____

_____

_____

Anecdotal records. Teachers should maintain anecdotal records for each student that include a brief description of each student as he or she reads orally or silently. Following is the information to be recorded:

■ What observations can be made about the use of strategies?

■ Can the student retell or summarize a passage after reading?

■ What are the strengths or weaknesses observed?

Figure 3.3

Student Literacy Observations

J. Camp has difficulty with understanding vocabulary. Impacts success on tests and understanding of text. Concept Definition Maps seem to help performance and understanding.

These brief descriptive recordings are helpful to jog a teacher's memory of individual student abilities and can be used along with student work when the student support team is trying to develop a plan for improving student achievement. Figure 3.3 is an anecdotal record used by a ninth grade biology teacher.

Reading logs or portfolios are excellent tools to gain a better understanding of a student's literacy ability and interests. Logs can reveal what types of books students are reading; what thoughts, questions, or insights a student has about a reading selection; how much time is spent reading and the number of books read; and what reading goals have been set and achieved by the reader. Follow-up conferences between the student and the teacher to discuss the log or portfolio provide insightful data related to the student's choice of reading material and understanding of text. They can give direction to the teacher as to instructional strategies the student may need to improve the reading process.

Informal reading inventories provide information about word attack or identification skills, retelling skills, and comprehension skills. Teachers trained to administer this type of assessment can gain information on reading levels and a general indication of strengths and weaknesses.

J.E.B. Stuart High School

J.E.B. Stuart High School, located outside of Washington, DC, in the suburban bedroom community of Fairfax County, Virginia, is beating the statistical odds to achieve student success. Two-thirds of the students are second language learners, more than 54 percent are eligible for free and reduced-price meals, and the school has an excessively high mobility rate and a high student diversity level. Mel Riddile, school principal, provides an intriguing vignette of his school's journey from the bottom of the achievement heap to the pinnacle of academic success. How did the school move from one of the lowest achieving schools within the Fairfax County School District to a school recognized as a Breakthrough High School? The answer, though not simple, is embedded in the school's actions to achieve literacy for all.

Eight years ago, J.E.B. Stuart High School students were clearly identified as some of the lowest performers in the school system on Virginia's Standards of Learning end-of-course exams. (See Figure 3.4.) Mel Riddile arrived on the scene as the new principal, and he candidly asked the staff, "What do we need to do to improve student achievement?" The staff provided two focus areas that have been critical to developing a solution for turning the learning opportunities around for students. First, the low attendance rate had to be turned around. Students were missing an average of 23 days per school year. This agonizing statistic has improved to an average of 7 days missed per year according to 2003 school data. Secondly, teachers stressed that students had to be taught to read well enough to pass content standards required in each of the school's core content classes. In other words, students had to be moved from functional literacy to academic proficiency. The two areas of focus provided by Stuart's staff served as the foundation of the school improvement plan.

Assessment Used to Guide Original Planning

Assessment provides the road map, or the big picture, to plan the journey for literacy improvement. Based on the recommendations of expert evaluators, Stuart staff chose to administer the Gates-MacGinitie Reading Test to all eighth graders entering the ninth grade at Stuart. This assessment tool was chosen because it is normed on English language learners and students of poverty, and it was recommended as a relevant test for the student population of Stuart. At first, there was resistance by district officials because they could not see the benefit of testing all eighth grade students scheduled to enter ninth grade at Stuart. That resistance was overcome, and the test was administered. The scores revealed some disturbing facts about the literacy levels of the prospective ninth graders.

As the data were analyzed, 76 percent of the students scored one standard deviation below grade level, and 25 percent of the students scored three years below grade level. Although the test indicated a problem, it did not provide the exact literacy deficit. Therefore, additional testing was required. An individual literacy inventory, Burns and Roe, was given to all students scoring below the 40th percentile on the Gates-MacGinitie. This follow-up assessment diagnosed specific literacy problems and helped the staff to develop an action plan to address the targeted literacy deficits.

Profile

J.E.B. Stuart High School

3301 Peace Valley Lane
Falls Church, VA 22044

Principal:
Dr. Mel J. Riddile

- *1,500 students*
- *Hispanic: 31 percent, white: 31 percent, Asian/other: 24 percent, black: 13 percent*
- *54 percent free and reduced-price meals*
- *97 percent annual graduation rate*
- *93 percent college admissions rate*
- *Recognitions: NASSP Breakthrough High School*

Figure 3.4

Performance of J.E.B. Stuart High School Students on the Virginia Standards of Learning Tests, 1998 and 2004

	1998	2004		1998	2004
Reading and Literature	64%	94%	World Studies II	62%	78%
Writing	73%	93%	U.S. and Virginia History	50%	96%
Algebra I	48%	87%	Biology	55%	81%
Geometry	63%	93%	Chemistry	46%	83%
Algebra II	55%	94%	Earth Science	68%	83%
World Studies I	60%	84%			

Scheduling and Additional Classes Provide Needed Instructional Support

The assessment results led to a reorganization of the schedule and class offerings at Stuart. A required literacy class was developed for all incoming ninth graders. Pre and post assessments are given to each student to document progress. The class is fluid in nature because the identified literacy needs of students are different. Some students require extra explicit instruction to develop required literacy skills, while other students move quickly through the computer-assisted lessons to more advanced literacy activities. The important aspect of this ninth grade literacy lab is that it is designed to meet the literacy needs of all students struggling to advance.

The students with the most critical literacy deficits are scheduled in an elective class that is taught by a literacy specialist. The specialist understands the specific literacy requirements of individual students and quickly develops a program to move students forward. The specialist provides explicit instruction in strategies at the literacy level of the student and additionally provides instruction with literacy strategies to read content texts such as history and science textbooks.

In addition to the computer lab and the elective reading class, students receive reinforcement with textbook literacy across the curriculum. A literacy coach was hired to work with all content teachers to support learning of literacy instructional strategies. Students receive individualized help in the lab and reading class, while content-area teachers employ literacy strategies before and during content instruction. Individual students who need additional support attend an after-school tutorial that meets three days per week, and there is also a summer school class to support literacy learning of students. If needed, students participate in a Level II literacy class as 10th graders. Student failure is not an option at J.E.B. Stuart High School.

Professional Development Encourages Changes in Instructional Program

Riddile indicated the most opposition to a secondary literacy program did not come from students or parents. The greatest resistance was among the teaching staff. First, teachers could not understand how they could cover course content and teach literacy strategies. Second, the teachers had no training in teaching literacy strategies. However, the data became key to convincing the staff there was a need to make a dramatic change from the traditional way of teaching to a more explicit form of teaching to meet the learning needs of students.

To turn teacher thinking around, initial professional development began with a 15-session college credit course. Three sessions, two hours each, were totally dedicated to literacy immersion strategies at the secondary level. The literacy coach supported teacher learning through mini-professional development sessions during the teacher's planning periods. Peer teaching opportunities with a write-up of observations were followed with teacher reflections and discussions of the peer learning experience. The process involved the literacy coach modeling the strategy; peer observations, feedback, and follow-up; and additional coaching and support if required. Riddile reiterated that data were the key to convincing everyone of the need to change, and the conscientious staff took responsibility to ensure that instructional changes were in place to lead to student success.

A school culture to support literacy continues to evolve at Stuart. The initial interpretation of the data and professional development to address learning needs of students and teachers began the process. Originally, teachers added a core repertoire of 15 literacy strategies that were fully immersed into instruction. All new teachers receive professional development to learn these core strategies. Today, experienced teachers add even more complex strategies to their daily instruction. Teachers at Stuart use a modified Madeline Hunter and Calvin Rosenshine Instructional Model that they call BEEP, "Beginning, Engaging, Ending, and Practicing." Embedded within this instructional model are pre, during, and post literacy strategies.

Communication with Elementary and Middle Schools to Expand Literacy Instruction Results in Better Prepared High School Students

Along with the focus for increased teacher and student learning at Stuart is an effort to continue and to expand literacy instruction at the elementary and middle school levels. Communication among staff at the three levels has identified the need to continue literacy instruction beyond the third grade. Riddile described this communication as having a profound impact on student literacy because students are arriving better prepared to succeed at the secondary level. Because the students often do not come from literacy-rich backgrounds, it is critical to maintain early success by continuing exposure to literacy-rich environments and literacy instruction beyond early elementary instruction.

Focus on Literacy Has Led Stuart Students to Success

It appears the administration and staff at J.E.B. Stuart High School have discovered the critical mix of leadership, assessment, professional development, targeted instruction, and explicit assessment-driven intervention to improve student learning and literacy. As Riddile stresses, it requires "a long-term commitment to building capacity of staff by using student data to drive the process that leads to success." It is an ongoing process that provides the structure for evaluation, reflection, action, and success.

Believing that all students can learn and maintaining high expectations for student success are the critical components of literacy instruction and improved student learning. Stuart students in 1998 were passing only one of the Virginia Standards of Learning tests. Today, Stuart students are exceeding Virginia's pass rate on all 11 exams. Even more astonishing, students are actually enrolling in the International Baccalaureate (IB) program at a higher rate than ever expected. In fact, many students who began with literacy intervention classes graduate with a number of the IB classes in their academic portfolio. Can students beat the odds of low literacy achievement and resulting academic failure? The answer is a resounding YES! Students at J.E.B. Stuart High School are definitely beating all odds.

4 Professional Development: The Recipe for Success

Building a school that truly values the individual student requires a form of professional development not traditionally practiced in most secondary schools. This situation becomes more complex as many secondary content-area teachers feel their teaching duties should remain within their field of expertise and consistently express their lack of preparation to teach literacy skills within their content area (Phillips, 2002). Yet, for a school to build capacity to support adolescent literacy, it must have the framework in place to provide the identified professional development needs. Since the old system of one-shot staff development activities has not proven effective, today's school leaders must foster an environment that supports ongoing professional development designed to give content teachers the instructional skills necessary to integrate literacy strategies into their daily instruction.

There is a strong correlation between high-quality professional development and student achievement. However, professional development is not a one-size-fits-all proposition; it must be targeted to the specific needs of the school population. An inner-city school in Chicago will have vastly different needs than a small school located in an isolated region of Alaska.

Research uses several adjectives to describe a high-quality professional development plan—collaborative, relevant, job-embedded, and collegial. To achieve effective professional development, teachers must be involved in the creation of the school's plan; their input is vital in assuring that the activities are relevant to both their needs and the needs of their students. To cause a significant change in a teacher's instructional practices, any professional growth effort must be directly applicable to the classroom and provide teachers with the necessary tools to implement challenging learning opportunities for their students. And finally, a collegial atmosphere must permeate the school to encourage teachers to discuss their professional practices and share their experiences with one another.

The principal plays a significant role in the school's journey to improve literacy. To ensure that professional development is sustained and ongoing, the principal must see that it is infused into the school climate and that staff members regularly participate in discussions of professional articles, form interest-based study groups, share strategies learned at conferences or workshops, and engage in discussions regarding the best literacy practices for adolescents.

The Learning First Alliance, a partnership of 12 education organizations, developed and publicized guidelines for assisting teachers with improving literacy instruction and ultimately teacher instruction. Some of the tenets for professional development to improve literacy include (a) involving all stakeholders; (b) linking student standards, curricular frameworks, textbooks, instructional programs, and assessments; (c) including professional development as a part of the professional's workday; (d) relying on expertise of colleagues, mentors, and other experts for professional development; (e) presence of a strong instructional leader; and finally, (f) long-range planning with enough funding to fully implement the professional development goals (Learning First Alliance, 1998).

Professional Development: Ten Action Steps for the Literacy Leader

---

1. Work closely with the Literacy Leadership Team to determine professional learning needs of teachers.

Professional development is one of the greatest tools available to improve student achievement. Through research-based professional development, teacher knowledge is increased and instructional strategies and skills are improved. The principal and the LLT need to ensure the school does not use a haphazard approach to improving instruction, but rather an approach based on assessment data.

They should begin by analyzing student achievement data to gauge strengths and weaknesses. Through a variety of formal and informal assessment tools (teacher surveys, interest surveys, observations, staff professional preparation data, etc.), they should next determine topics for staff growth. By meshing student and staff needs, a plan for the professional growth component of the school's literacy improvement plan can be developed. Once the tentative professional development plan has been developed, it should be shared with the staff and, based on their input, revised where necessary.

Any plan for professional development must be evaluated on an ongoing basis. Tools for evaluating the plan should be put in place so that the plan can be easily revised if student achievement does not improve. Additionally, strategies must be in place to evaluate the implementation and effectiveness of literacy strategies used within the classroom.

The LLT must meet often to evaluate progress and determine what revisions are necessary to the professional development plan. A yearly evaluation is simply not adequate to fully gauge the effectiveness of the program. Just as student progress within the classroom must be consistently monitored, so must the professional development plan and its impact upon instruction be assessed in an ongoing fashion to evaluate if and how teachers are benefiting from the staff development program.

Suggested questions for evaluating the plan include the following:

- Are teachers implementing instructional strategies to improve literacy within their content area?

- Are all teachers participating fully in staff development opportunities?

- Is student achievement improving based on acquired use of literacy strategies they have learned in literacy-savvy classrooms?

2. Identify and capitalize on staff members' talents and interests to support the ongoing, job-embedded professional learning.

Teachers learn from one another, and school leaders must encourage and nurture professional dialogue, powerful conversations, and opportunities for teachers to share their knowledge and talents. Early in the planning stages of any literacy improvement plan, the school should use interest surveys or similar tools to assess areas of teacher expertise and willingness to serve as a resource for their fellow teachers.

Often, quality sharing among teachers does not take place naturally. An effective leader creates opportunities for teachers to learn from each other and to share best practices through activities such as shared teaching. The quietest member of the staff may evolve as the best resource for others if given the opportunity to shine. Principals, like teachers, must work to develop cooperative learning teams. Time set aside each month during scheduled faculty meetings provides an ideal setting for the cooperative teams to discuss content-area literacy strategies. Teacher leaders within each team can lead the discussion or activities.

The literacy specialist/coach, along with content-area teachers, can often lead many of the professional development activities within the school setting. What better way for a math teacher to learn how to apply literacy strategies in the math class than from a fellow math teacher?

The principal and leadership team must identify and encourage teachers to learn from one another. Two ways this can be done are by using the weekly newsletter to highlight a teacher's successful use of an instructional literacy strategy within class or by giving a Certificate of Excellence each week to teachers who have been observed using best-practice literacy strategies.

Recognition of teacher literacy leaders will begin professional dialogues among the teaching staff. The school leader must encourage these dialogues that promote job-embedded, standards-based learning from each another. Teachers learn best from one another, but it is the administrator's responsibility to assure that teachers have time during the workday to develop this valuable resource.

Administrators should ensure that each teacher feels valued by recognizing and nurturing their strengths. Teachers who feel empowered are willing to share their knowledge in professional learning activities. Sometimes, the best professional development happens when we rely on teachers to creatively use their skills as a resource for helping other teachers in the improvement process.

3. Implement shared teaching or other forms of coaching to learn and immerse literacy strategies within content classes.

Shared teaching was developed out of the peer-coaching model and is a successful practice supported by the ARI (2004). It provides an opportunity for teachers to share strategies with confidential feedback, support, and assistance. Two teachers work together and select a time when one teacher can visit the host teacher's classroom to view a literacy strategy being immersed into the instruction. Shared teaching allows the visiting teacher to observe and learn a new instructional skill, provide feedback on teacher actions and student engagement, and ask questions about the implementation of the strategy. An opportunity for collaborative reflection follows the shared teaching activity.

The steps of shared teaching include (1) discussing the planned lesson (preconference), (2) teaching or taking notes (observation), and (3) discussing and reflecting on the lesson (postconference). Shared teaching is:

- Specific, not general

- Professional, not social

- Collegial, not competitive

- Helping, not evaluating

- Confidential, not public

- Future oriented and dynamic, not static (ARI, 2004).

Other formats of shared teaching include peer coaching and mentor coaching. The peer-coaching strategy is a three-step process where teachers

- Observe demonstrations of a new literacy skill

- Practice the new skill with the peer coach supporting efforts and clarifying skill implementation

- Give and receive feedback that is specific and nonevaluative.

Follow-up sessions encourage teachers to reflect on instructional practices, collaboratively solve instructional issues, plan future lessons, and analyze curricula to determine which learning strategies will best support the learning.

Mentor coaching includes support by a literacy coach, master teacher, or other staff developer. Teachers implement strategies learned in a professional development session and are then given the support of a professional facilitator. This type of coaching is especially effective for new teachers. Mentor coaching includes steps closely identified with shared teaching and peer coaching:

- Skill demonstration

- Classroom observation by the mentor teacher

- Follow-up reflection and analysis of skill implementation (Strickland, 2004).

---

4. Encourage professional "talk" among staff and provide time for discussions.

Teachers learn so much from one another when they have the opportunity to discuss a professional book or article. Having a focused literacy conversation is an invaluable tool for professional growth.

Just like students, teachers learn best through active engagement, analyzing and thinking about teaching, and talking about successful strategies. The opportunity to engage staff in discussions regarding their instructional practices is an aspect of professional growth that is often overlooked. Therefore, because teachers learn most effectively when they are actively engaged as learners of new strategies, a savvy administrator will provide opportunities for teachers to share, analyze, and learn from one another—and the greatest beneficiaries are the students.

As the instructional leader, assure that teachers have time during the weekly schedule to:

- Participate in professional discussions or book talks

- Observe instructional demonstrations by master teachers

- Focus on best literacy practices
- Discuss problems and solutions of content-area reading instructional strategies.

5. Conduct a Literacy Walk to identify professional development needs.

A Literacy Walk is a valuable professional development tool that helps teachers and the LLT focus on the successful implementation of strategic literacy teaching within the content area. Members of the Literacy Walk team may vary, but there should be some consistency so that trends and needs can be identified. A Literacy Walk helps teachers observe how other teachers are integrating literacy strategies into the daily instruction. This practice helps to encourage "powerful conversations" among the staff related to literacy instructional practices (Gassenheimer, 2003).

As the team walks through classrooms, it should focus on looking for one particular behavior. Members simply tally the behaviors observed on a small notepad. (See Figure 4.1.)

6. Actively seek and provide resources for professional learning.

Limited funding for professional development is often an issue for many school administrators. However, some of the poorest schools and districts have developed strategies for wisely using available funds and seeking additional funding. Additional information related to public and corporate funding may be found in Chapter 2, action step 7.

7. Participate in professional learning activities.

A professional learning activity will likely be met with resistance if faculty members attend while the principal remains in the office. If the principal's desire is to inspire teachers to change and improve literacy opportunities for all students, then he or she must be totally committed to learning from professional development activities. When teachers observe their leader's commitment to learning best literacy practices, then motivation increases to improve and participate in professional learning activities.

Like teachers, most administrators do not have an in-depth understanding of adolescent literacy needs and best practices. Learning adolescent literacy strategies, content-area reading strategies, and how to help teachers improve requires participation in professional development activities. Otherwise, how will the principal become the literacy instructional leader at his or her school?

8. Use classroom observations to identify and support ongoing professional development needs.

As the school instructional leader and chief advocate for professional development, it is critical that the principal be in classrooms daily to observe and encourage the full implementation of literacy strategy instruction. The principal's presence should not be used as a "caught you" visit, but one that is dedicated to improving the learning

Figure 4.1

A Literacy Walk Sample

Literacy Walk

Objective: Find evidence of literacy strategy integration in content classes.

Number of times observed	Strategy	Examples
I I I	Prereading	Observed brainstorm, Concept Definition Map, What's in a Picture?
I I I	During Reading	Data chart, Semantic Map, Question/answer/response
I I	Postreading	Magnet Summary, Team report of findings

Results of Walk: Visited 10 classrooms.
Literacy strategies used in 8 out of 10 classes.

A Literacy Walk is composed of four essential parts:

Preparation. Team members identify the literacy evidence to observe as they conduct the *Walk.* The strategy to observe may be (1) teacher instructional behavior, (2) student engagement/work, and (3) environmental evidence of literacy instruction.

Class walk. Members spend 5 to 10 minutes in each classroom to observe visible evidence of the literacy focus. They use a tally on a checklist or small notepad to record evidence of literacy instruction and learning.

Assessment of evidence. The team reassembles to evaluate visible evidence of literacy emphasis and implementation. The tallies are analyzed, and evidence that literacy instruction and literacy are actually immersed within the classroom is discussed. If a walk through 10 classrooms results in evidence of only one literacy strategy, then that is an indicator that literacy integration is not being implemented in a way to help students achieve success. This quick, informal assessment helps make informed decisions related to professional development and improvement of the instructional program.

Collaborative feedback and planning. Opportunities are provided for feedback, reflection, discussion, and interpretation of observable behaviors. If done in a nonthreatening way, this approach will spark conversations related to literacy instruction efforts and provide opportunities for teacher modeling, shared teaching, and professional discussions related to improving content teaching strategies through embedded pre, during, and post literacy strategies (ARI, 2004).

of students, as well as teachers. Observations should provide answers to the following questions:

- Are teachers embedding literacy strategies in the instruction?

- Are teachers modeling the use of literacy strategies?

- Are teachers helping students to make connections by using literacy strategies before, during, and after the lesson?

- Are teachers activating prior knowledge before giving a reading assignment?

- Are teachers using strategies that fully develop students' metacognition?

- Are teachers providing opportunities for students to read?

- Are teachers providing time for shared reading activities?

- Are teachers encouraging read-alouds and follow-up student conferences to discuss text?

- Are teachers providing time for student reflection about what they have read through the use of journals, logs, or other reflective activities?

- Are teachers modeling and encouraging the connection between reading and writing?

- Are teachers developing higher-order thinking skills in students by asking them to read critically?

- Are students using literacy strategies independently to get meaning from the text?

Follow-up conferences with the teacher can lead to discussions that identify additional professional learning needs and strategies for improvement.

---

9. Creatively schedule blocks of time to assure ongoing professional learning.

Professional staff are often disinclined to stay after school for professional development. The complaints are almost nonceasing and the practice is self-defeating. To truly provide an environment for literacy improvement, options within the regular schedule of the school day must be explored to provide time for teachers to discuss, plan, and learn to improve the literacy program.

There are many ways to plan time for professional development:

- When planning the schedule during the spring, explore options that schedule time for interdisciplinary teams or departmental planning. These chunks of time can be used for teacher collaboration and learning literacy strategies. It may take several runs of the schedule, but time can be created in the regular schedule for professional development.

- Look at other chunks of time during the day. Can the lunch period be utilized for student support teams or departmental learning teams? Paraprofessionals or parent volunteers may work with the administration to release groups of teachers from duties in order to attend professional learning sessions.

- Plan for half-day departmental and interdisciplinary team professional development sessions. Substitutes can be scheduled far ahead of this activity, allowing the staff to attend the sessions while substitutes assume their responsibilities. This works best when the substitute is scheduled for two days and rotates in to assist with four different teachers' classrooms.

- Work closely with district personnel to schedule staff development days within the district schedule. Look for optimum times for professional development and ways that district staff can work together to improve districtwide literacy efforts. Local professional development can also be scheduled into these days. Delayed starts or early releases are another option to explore at the district level.

Collaboration between the district and school levels can lead to creative scheduling to improve student literacy. If the literacy effort is not a district initiative, then work closely with your district leaders to communicate your needs for professional development time.

---

10. Monitor assessment data and work with the LLT to analyze the ongoing learning needs of teachers.

After implementing cognitive literacy strategies across the content areas, questions must be asked to evaluate the effectiveness of the program. These include:

- Is the data being used to inform the staff about student progress and teacher knowledge related to best practices of reading instruction?

- Do teachers view the professional learning program as improving or impacting the way they teach literacy strategies within their content areas?

- What does action research reveal about student progress within classrooms where specific literacy strategies have been implemented?

- What continued needs for professional learning development do the assessment data identify?

Based on teacher input, the LLT should determine what staff development activities have been most effective, what steps are needed to improve staff development activities, and what types of staff development will be required to satisfy additional professional learning needs of the staff. This information should then be used to modify, add, and/or delete activities from the professional development plan.

And Remember...

- The administrator's goal is to use every opportunity to magnify teacher success and build a collaborative learning community. This encourages each staff member to learn content-area literacy strategies from their peers' strengths and skills.

- The principal leads the way. A principal who is not an active participant in staff development sessions will not see a marked improvement in the teaching abilities of the staff or in the students' literacy achievement scores.

- Principals who work to provide adequate time for professional development are going to win the support of the staff and will ultimately realize increased student achievement as a result.

- Staff members must buy into all plans for improvement. If the plan is developed without staff input and acceptance, it is just another plan on the shelf. Staff involvement is critical to identifying needs through surveys, self-evaluations, and knowledge of possible presenters for professional learning activities. It is a wise administrator who fully considers assessment data, committee suggestions, and staff input before implementing any professional development plan.

CREATING A CULTURE OF LITERACY: A GUIDE FOR MIDDLE AND HIGH SCHOOL PRINCIPALS

Learn More About It: What the Experts and Research Say About Professional Development

Successful professional development connects curriculum with assessment, instruction, and professional development. Instructional programs that result in measurable student achievement are based on sound professional development opportunities (Darling-Hammond, 1997; Wenglinsky, 2001). According to King and Newman (2000, p. 376), professional development has the most impact on teacher performance if teachers can "concentrate on instruction and student outcomes in the specific contexts in which they teach." King and Newman additionally suggest professional development becomes relevant when teachers are permitted to work with peers and have a connection to researchers and program developers.

Nancy Raiche (2000) emphasizes three areas of professional development for secondary teachers: instructional strategies, collaborative planning and development, and course management. Gaskins (1998, p. 210) says that staff development should be "ongoing, collaborative and in-depth as it engages teachers and support staff in exploring and understanding research-based principles and theories about instruction, curriculum and cognition." Ian MacDonald (2001) suggests that professional development models must go beyond the one-day exposure to new ideas and further supports the above contention. He states, "Without an understanding of when and why methods should be used, and a framework of necessary educational principles to support this decision making, most teachers revert quickly to previous practice" (p. 156).

Effective staff development opportunities provide teachers with the necessary tools to implement challenging learning opportunities for their students. In a commentary for *Reading Today,* Darcy Bradley (1998) stresses that skillful instruction requires teachers to have multiple approaches to teaching and to know how to group students for learning.

Successful staff development programs use direct classroom observations to offer sustained support for implementing strategies learned at staff development sessions (Gibbons and Kimmell, 1997; King and Newman, 2000). In one program sponsored by the Center for Pre-college Programs of the New Jersey Institute of Technology (Gibbons and Kimmell, 1997), weekly classroom visits were encouraged as follow-up, and graduate assistants modeled standards-based effective instructional methods.

In a study by Reys et al. (1997), several essential characteristics of an effective staff development program are identified. The authors conclude that a successful professional development program should be at least two years in duration. Technical assistance should be available for teachers as they begin to implement newly learned strategies. A collegial atmosphere should exist so teachers can share experiences with one another. Teachers should have the opportunity to reflect on their teaching practices and make changes as needed. Professional growth activities should be based on current research in successful classroom practices.

Teacher networks that offer substantive feedback and support are a suggested framework for successful professional development (Pennell and Firestone, 1998). Success revolves around teachers getting together to share successful teaching strategies and to discuss specific problems they may be experiencing in the classroom. Within the teacher networks, the educators have an opportunity to concentrate on "particular subject areas, teaching methods, or approaches to reform that give members a common purpose; a significant part of the leadership for the efforts comes from teachers themselves" (p. 354). Teacher professional development networks encourage teacher access to a variety of resources, ongoing support, and leadership opportunities; and networks also limit the extreme costs of the more traditional professional development opportunities.

To be effective, professional development must be based on standards and be assessment driven. Traditional one-shot workshops do not provide teachers with the necessary tools to change instructional habits within their specific theaters of instructional practice. Although the speaker may be dynamic, the actual change in classroom instruction does not usually occur once the initial excitement about the presentation has dissolved. Professional development must create a connection between the teacher's learning and increased student achievement (Sparks and Hirsh, 1997). Professional development with the most impact provides a framework for teachers to evaluate their instructional practices, generate new stratagems for instruction, and evaluate their instructional practices on student achievement (Kelleher, 2003).

Schools that are making successful strides toward changing professional development programs based on National Staff Development Council standards are engaging in powerful conversations (PCs) related to local professional development plans. In Alabama, some school faculties are engaged in PCs to critically assess the overall effectiveness of the staff development program. Sample questions that faculties ask are:

- Does our staff development plan grow out of a careful analysis of student achievement results and other performance data—broken out by race, socioeconomic status, gender, and special needs?

- Are most or all of our staff development dollars invested in strategies that will improve teacher performance and raise student achievement?

- Is our staff development tied to the real work of our teachers—to authentic issues they are grappling with in their classrooms today?

- Do we avoid one-time workshops and other staff development that includes no follow-up support for teachers as they try out new skills and strategies?

- Do we take advantage of the professional expertise in our own school and encourage our teachers to share special skills and knowledge?

- Is it common for teachers in our school to exchange ideas, try out new strategies together, and do action research to find promising approaches to instructional problems?

- Is professional learning always going on in our school, as teachers talk in the halls, observe one another in classrooms, meet in teams and departments, and pass along effective teaching strategies? (Norton, 2003)

Cathy Gassenheimer of the Alabama Best Practices Center commends schools that use the Powerful Conversations Model to improve staff development practices because those schools engaging "in rich, guided conversations" have experienced "dramatic results" (Gassenheimer, 2003).

The research and recommendations suggest the importance of professional development sessions that prepare teachers to integrate literacy strategies into their daily instruction. Ongoing professional training to understand current student data and instructional skills to support learning requirements of students are the goals of high-quality of professional development (National Staff Development Council, 2001). Scheduling during the day allows teachers to work together in collaborative teams to focus on ways to improve instruction in the classroom. Time should permit opportunities for teachers to observe master teachers who use explicit strategies to improve comprehension within the various content areas. Teachers require time to reflect and work with one another to solidify effective instructional practices that improve reading opportunities for students. Workshop presenters may include professional presenters, peers, university staff, and others who can focus on the required needs of the professional staff.

Duncan Polytechnical High School

Duncan Polytechnical High School in Fresno, CA, is well deserving of NASSP Breakthrough High School recognition, and Principal Carol Hansen glowingly shares a rich story of teacher and student success. During the 1980s, Duncan would have been described as an occupational training school for dropouts or nonacademic students seeking the basics of a vocation. Today Duncan is a vocational specialization school that encourages high academic expectations for all with improved literacy opportunities at the very heart of the transition. Students at Duncan not only learn specialized vocational skills, they also study a curriculum that supports academic rigor and preparation for community or four-year colleges.

Duncan students have demonstrated success by meeting the California academic performance index targets as well as the federal yearly progress goals. In fact, the school has surpassed seven other schools within the Fresno Unified School District and is one of the highest achieving schools in California. Duncan students are exceeding all expectations, an outstanding accomplishment considering that 91 percent qualify for free and reduced-price meals and 34 percent are identified as second language learners. Another achievement for Duncan is that 82 percent of their 10th graders pass the California tests for mathematics and reading/language arts. Students enrolled in advanced placement courses have increased from zero in the 2001 academic year to 101 for 2004–05.

How the transition occurred at Duncan is a modern marvel of collaboration, professional development, teacher commitment to student success, and an academic program personalized to meets the needs of all students.

Change Begins with Collaboration

Hansen's philosophy is "people close to the issues need to make the decisions," so site-based management at Duncan encourages shared decision making and the participation of all stakeholders in every aspect of the school improvement process. Collaborative decisions have impacted all areas of the school's program, from creating the school schedule to developing a highly effective instructional program. This culture of shared decision making and co-ownership for school improvement has fostered an amazing collegial effort to support student success.

Teachers at Duncan recognized that a student's ability to read and write well was the very foundation of understanding technical manuals and preparing for a successful vocational career after high school. When the data indicated many students arrived with poor literacy skills, the staff quickly reached consensus that students would require additional support to graduate with solid vocational and academic skills. Working together, the staff developed a school improvement plan that was directed toward each student successfully completing a rigorous vocational and academic program.

Professional Development Provides the Glue

At Duncan, the collaborative professional development process began under the leadership of the principal. A careful analysis of student data revealed a stark need to focus on literacy, and teacher professional learning needs were targeted to address the issue. The

Profile

Duncan Polytechnical High School

4330 E. Garland Ave. Fresno, CA 93726

Principal: Carol G. Hansen

- *1,023 students*
- *Grades 9–12*
- *57.9 percent Asian, 32 percent Hispanic, 6.7 percent white, 2.9 percent black, 0.5 percent other*
- *91 percent free and reduced-price meals*
- *97 percent annual graduation rate*
- *Recognitions: NASSP Breakthrough High School and California Distinguished School*

initial professional development began small. During the first year of the plan, departmental groups began to learn strategies to support effective use of the textbooks. This small group evolved into a schoolwide effort to learn successful literacy strategies and to fully integrate these strategies into the content areas.

There is a strong connection between reading and writing, so the centerpiece for the second target of professional development was writing. Eleven teachers attended a week of intensive professional development at the San Joaquin Valley Writing Project sponsored by Fresno State University. The attendees, armed with new ideas and strategies to improve writing, returned to Duncan to share with other staff members. Through collaborative efforts, an action plan was designed to fully integrate writing across the curriculum.

To support the inclusion of reading and writing across the content areas, the administration designated a lead literacy teacher. Although not a literacy coach, this individual had a successful track record of literacy integration. The literacy leader's main responsibility was to model successful practices for other content-area teachers and to assist with integration of reading and writing strategies throughout the school.

Teachers at Duncan have a one-hour lunch block, but 30 minutes of the block are dedicated to professional development. During summer professional days, the teachers and administration carefully analyze student data and plan professional development to support student achievement. The lead literacy teacher works closely with the other teachers to model literacy strategies during the lunchtime professional development period. She also works closely with the Title I teacher to determine the instructional needs of students, and this becomes a basis for professional development opportunities. Every aspect of the professional development program is driven by the instructional needs of the students. At Duncan, falling through the cracks is not an option.

Personalized Instructional Program

The staff also recognized the need to personalize instruction to support academic success. When Duncan students first enter the school, they are given a strong foundation in mathematics, reading, and language arts. The foundation begins by providing students with technological literacy skills as well as the technical and analytical writing skills required for success. Through the structures developed by a caring, supportive staff, students learn to communicate effectively through a comprehensive portfolio development and presentations. Students gain confidence through this process, at the same time learning important communication skills they will need for future success. At Duncan, Hansen indicates, teachers never say, "I am not a teacher of reading" because they fully understand the importance of integrating literacy strategies into daily instruction of core content standards.

Silent Sustained Reading (SSR) is a daily activity at Duncan that is built into the schedule; students have 20 minutes at the end of first period each day to self-select books of interest for literacy. Teachers model reading and are not involved with other activities during this dedicated reading time. The administrators even take time to visit at least one class per week to share in SSR time with students.

Students are given many instructional supports to achieve academic success. A Summer Bridge Program provides orientation that helps students successfully transition from middle school to high school. Ninth graders needing additional support have the opportunity to take a reading class that prepares them for advanced expository text reading and college-level reading. There are extended learning opportunities, tutorial labs, and a seventh-period intervention class for students requiring additional assistance. Second language learners participate in a companion reading class specifically designed to meet their individual literacy needs. Many of the students maintain a heavy workload outside of school, so teachers open their classrooms for tutoring before school and during lunch. Every effort is made to support students because Duncan's goal is for all students to graduate from high school prepared to enter a community or four-year college and succeed in their chosen career paths.

Professional Commitment Ensures Student Success

Visionary leadership, committed instructors, and a common goal to support student success are critical keys to Duncan's accomplishments. Because of a collaborative staff that uses assessment to drive instructional practices, students at Duncan are achieving higher and higher academic success.

The achievement of the Duncan students is a result of the school's leadership and staff deciding to make literacy immersion a cornerstone of their program. Collaboratively they identified the need and developed a game plan to address the issues. And the efforts are paying off—Duncan has a 97 percent graduation rate, the majority of the students go on to postsecondary programs, and 18 percent of its graduates complete at least a baccalaureate degree. This is a school that is truly fulfilling its promise of literacy achievement to its students.

School Profile 3:
Duncan Polytechnic High School

5 Highly Effective Teachers: The Essential Ingredient of a Literacy Program

There is no more important step a principal can take to encourage literacy for all students than to ensure each child has access to highly effective teachers. Survey results of 8th and 12th graders on the 1998 NAEP indicated students were more likely to score higher on the assessment if their teachers held them accountable for literacy performance and understanding (Donahue et al., 1999).

Unfortunately, highly skilled teachers do not magically appear right out of teacher preparation programs, but rather, with the proper care and feeding, grow in effectiveness over time. However, the good news is support systems such as peer coaching and shared teaching can be successfully used to produce highly effective teachers who use strategic teaching skills.

A successful literacy program takes the combined effort of skilled content-area teachers and reading specialists/coaches. Together, these teachers, along with other specialized teachers, can identify reading problems and aggressively attack the deficiency if they are given the proper tools for success, such as professional development, materials, and positive support.

Content-Area Teachers

Perhaps there is no one individual with a greater impact on the secondary student's quest for literacy than the content-area teacher. The most effective of these teachers focus directly on the critical reading needs of the students by teaching specific strategies to understand the often-difficult expository text found in science and history books. These strategies must be used **daily** to help students think critically about the text, analyze the written word, and build connections between the text and their lives. Therefore, the sooner secondary teachers are helped to make the paradigm shift from "I teach a content area" to "I am a reading teacher in my content area," the quicker secondary students will be reading and comprehending at grade level.

It is no easy feat to be a highly effective content-area teacher. It requires an individual to possess both "kid connection" and instructional skills and use them in a manner that helps every student in the classroom become a successful learner. This teacher supports students' reading and understanding of text by skillfully integrating pre, during, and post literacy strategies into daily instruction. He or she understands the unique characteristics of adolescents, the ways in which they learn, and how to motivate them; this knowledge is then deftly used to craft daily lessons. Figure 5.1 depicts the characteristics of a highly effective, strategic teacher.

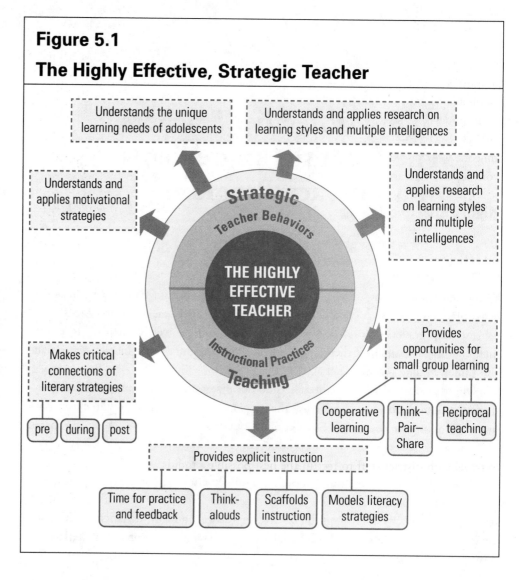

Figure 5.1

The Highly Effective, Strategic Teacher

Understands the unique learning needs of adolescents

Understands and applies research on learning styles and multiple intelligences

Understands and applies motivational strategies

Understands and applies research on learning styles and multiple intelligences

Strategic Teacher Behaviors

THE HIGHLY EFFECTIVE TEACHER

Instructional Practices Teaching

Makes critical connections of literary strategies

pre | during | post

Provides opportunities for small group learning

Cooperative learning | Think–Pair–Share | Reciprocal teaching

Provides explicit instruction

Time for practice and feedback | Think-alouds | Scaffolds instruction | Models literacy strategies

Literacy Specialist

The role of the literacy specialist has evolved from that of a teacher who works only with the struggling reader, to that of a specialist who supports the struggling reader through intensive evaluation and instruction and serves as a resource to the classroom teacher. The International Reading Association (IRA) defines the literacy specialist as one who:

- Provides assessment and specialized reading instruction
- Conducts professional development activities
- Establishes reading program goals with peers and helps peers to accomplish goals
- Defines and clarifies the literacy program to parents and community
- Exhibits appropriate reading strategies
- Shares current research and models best practices with faculty (IRA, 1998).

Today, four major roles of the literacy specialist should be considered as a literacy program is developed at the secondary level. Literacy specialists must provide leadership as they serve as a *coach* for the content-area teacher, an *assessment specialist,* an *instructional specialist,* and an *intervention specialist.*

Working within this framework, the literacy specialist's ability to work with colleagues and teach strategies to improve the school literacy program is a high priority. His or her role takes on new meaning when working with the teachers and the administrator to improve their knowledge about the teaching of literacy. The literacy specialist/coach conducts workshops, models literacy strategies, and provides guidance as the school literacy team develops strategies for individual students. It takes a special individual to work with all of the personalities of the school team, so it is critical the literacy specialist is someone who has not only a knowledge of literacy instruction but also the ability to work with adult learners.

Highly Effective Teachers: Eight Action Steps for the Literacy Leader

1. Hire the best teachers possible.

Hiring effective staff is possibly the most important job of the principal. By collaboratively working with existing staff to select highly skilled and motivated teachers, a principal can do much to enhance the literacy program of the school and therefore impact student academic success.

The interview process should reveal an insight into the candidate's philosophies, knowledge of content, instructional strategies, understanding of literacy concepts, classroom management, and a committed willingness to continue to grow professionally. Interview questions should require thought and provide the selection committee with an in-depth knowledge of the candidate's abilities. In some cases, it may be necessary to travel with district staff to recruit the best possible candidates for the school.

2. Generate excitement for change among the teaching staff.

As the school leader, the principal is the key to bringing staff on board to increase the literacy levels of all students. This role as an instructional leader is critical to assuring that students have access to highly effective teachers. The principal can build momentum and excitement for change by recognizing staff efforts in improving literacy, providing opportunities for professional growth and professional conversations, supporting teachers as they step outside their comfort zones to become literacy teachers within their content areas, and being a cheerleader for literacy improvement.

3. Establish specific and measurable goals for improving literacy.

Highly skilled teachers seek to improve their teaching practices. By setting schoolwide literacy goals, the principal can help create a focus that centers on teaching practices to improve student achievement. Setting specific and measurable goals related to increasing student literacy levels can provide a foundation for teacher motivation and accountability. When teachers take responsibility for their students' success and for improving their delivery of literacy instruction, they experience a sense of personal accomplishment. The principal's role is to work closely with the teaching staff to ensure this happens by, for example, building literacy improvement into teacher evaluations.

4. Ensure that curriculum is aligned with standards.

Often, excellent instruction is taking place within the classroom, but it is not related to standards or what should be taught on a K–12 continuum of skills for literacy. The principal must work with district office administration and the appropriate teaching staff to ensure this alignment is both completed and implemented. To increase the chances of this happening:

a. Work with teachers to closely examine the curriculum to determine if it supports the literacy program.

b. Visit classrooms to assure that every teacher is teaching to the aligned curriculum/standards.

c. Evaluate instructional materials to determine if they support both the curriculum and the literacy goals.

d. Regularly examine lesson plans to understand what is being taught and ask how you can help teachers to achieve their instructional goals. Teachers will appreciate your interest, support, and understanding of what they are attempting to accomplish within their classrooms.

e. Ensure that all teachers are teaching to the prescribed content standards. Teachers have individual strengths, but it is critical that they teach the same content to all students. While each student has their own learning style, ability, and may learn at different rates, they all should have equal access to content. Every student within the walls of the school must have equal opportunities to learn and achieve at high levels. This will not occur if teachers are allowed to teach to their own curriculum when they close the door to their classroom.

5. Ensure that content-area literacy strategies are used daily within classroom instruction.

Once teachers have the tools to improve literacy within their content area, they must begin to integrate these strategies into their daily instruction. Changing instructional habits is not easy, so the role of the administrator becomes clear. The principal becomes the cheerleader and the encourager as he or she supports teachers' efforts to change their delivery of instruction. The principal's involvement and emphasis on improving instruction will help the teachers improve their teaching strategies, as well as help them to feel valued for what they are doing to improve student achievement.

6. Evaluate the use of instructional strategies to improve literacy through the use of formal and informal observations.

Nothing impacts student achievement more than teachers who are skilled at using explicit instructional strategies to help students read and comprehend text. Teachers must use their knowledge of best practices to improve student learning, and as the instructional leader, the principal must assure that the best possible teaching is occurring within the classroom. Suggested practices and instructional skills the principal should look for during formal and informal observations include, but are not limited to, the following:

- Teachers have well-defined lesson plans that include measurable objectives with a plan for achieving them. Explicit strategies and activities should be identified.

- Teachers set high expectations for all students to learn **and** provide the scaffolding needed to meet those expectations.

- Prior knowledge is activated to set the stage for learning new content material.

- Teachers utilize instruction that is explicit, incorporating pre, during, and post literacy strategies to help activate prior knowledge, develop abilities in metacognition, and encourage higher-order thinking skills.

- Fully developed connections between reading and writing are emphasized.

- EVERY student is held accountable for learning, and various means are used to assess students' understanding of reading assignments.

- The use of research-based strategies enhances all learning styles and multiple intelligences. If students are not "getting it," then teachers should use a broad base of strategies within their "basket of tricks" to reteach and help all learners learn and achieve.

- Excellence is achieved in a classroom environment that is conducive to learning. Students should be actively engaged in the process and the teacher should not waste valuable class time. Student learning is promoted through encouragement and genuine concern about each student's literacy improvement program.

7. Exhibit courageous leadership in determining the need for staff changes.

As new teachers come on board, it is the principal's job to grow and develop them into highly skilled professionals. Methods to use include partnering them with master teachers as a mentor, providing suggestions to improve instruction through ongoing professional learning strategies, and giving them every opportunity to grow as an effective teacher. However, if a teacher remains ineffective, then the tough decision will need to be made to not renew a teacher's contract.

Always keep in mind that student achievement is the number-one priority. If a teacher is either unwilling or incapable of providing the best possible instruction for all students, then the responsibility falls on the administrator to recommend non-renewal. Depending on the state's and/or district's contract with their teachers, this action may be complicated (especially in the case of a teacher who is tenured or on a permanent contract) and require help of the district legal team. However, there is no excuse for not ensuring all students in the school are receiving the best possible instruction.

8. Collaborate closely with the literacy specialist/coach and the LLT to use assessment results to determine the professional development needed to ensure a highly skilled professional staff.

Encourage teacher involvement on the school literacy committee. Do not be afraid of sharing leadership with this valuable team; it will become the mover and shaker within the school culture to support change for adolescent literacy. This team, along with your help, is responsible for interpreting assessment data and using it to develop a professional development program based on the school's identified learning needs.

This committee's professional conversations for improvement will spread well beyond the walls of the meeting room. If the principal supports its efforts, this committee's work will serve as a stimulus for continued school improvement. Shared brainstorming based on data will result in an action plan for improvement that supports both the teachers and students.

Learn More About It: What the Experts and Research Say About Highly Effective Teachers

Content-Area Teachers

Content teachers are the best source to provide students with explicit instruction on how to critically think about the text (Abromitis, 1994; Campbell, 1994; Kamil et al., 2000). Teachers who model how to use a variety of graphic organizers help students find strategies to graphically organize the assigned text in order to develop a

---

And Remember...

■ The importance of hiring high-quality teachers cannot be overemphasized. However, in looking at the credentials of an applicant, be sure to investigate how well the individual can connect with the students he or she will be teaching. It is much easier to improve a teacher's instructional skills than it is to give him or her "kid connection" skills.

■ Work with the education department at the local university to encourage the provision of literacy training for preservice teachers. It will make university students better prepared to teach in the classroom and make them more desirable as potential employees for a school district.

■ Do not be afraid to confront a teacher who is unwilling to meet the expectations set by the school's literacy program. Students deserve teachers who choose to give them the best instruction possible.

■ Build confidence in those teachers who are trying, but struggling, to implement the new literacy program. It is not easy to change instructional habits. Look for signs of implementation, recognize their efforts, applaud their successes, and provide them with the support needed to make further gains.

■ Model literacy strategies when you present at staff and in-service meetings. Use strategies that build strong readers when the staff is asked to read and discuss a professional article. Demonstrate metacognition strategies by explaining how *you* thought about something you read. This not only helps teachers learn new skills, but highlights you as an instructional leader as well.

■ Your mission is to support the findings and recommendations of the literacy committee. It has put time and effort into analyzing data and researching best literacy practices to share with the staff. Your support validates its findings and efforts. By actively participating on this committee, you will assure that the road map for literacy improvement is well defined and the school is ready to make the journey to literacy success.

"picture" of the reading material. Demonstrating how to use textbook aides such as captions, bold print, and headings help both struggling and proficient readers gain a framework for thinking about and organizing their thoughts related to the reading. Effective teachers expand the use of these strategies by helping students develop a connection between reading and writing. When students write about the text read, they make the connections with the printed text and develop a clearer understanding of the printed word (Alvermann and Moore, 1991; Tierney and Pearson, 1992; Moje, Dillon, and O'Brien, 2000).

Highly effective secondary teachers, no matter the content they teach, effectively employ before reading, during reading, and after reading strategies. These teachers activate prior knowledge about a topic to help students begin thinking about the text and make connections with known information (Ausubel, 1968; Carey, Harste, and Smith, 1981; Henning, 1994, as cited in Manzo, 2001; Vacca and Vacca, 1999). Additionally, the skilled teacher will help students understand the vocabulary essential to the concept being taught by skimming the text to find new words, looking at bold print to find unidentified words, or using other strategies to identify and talk about new vocabulary. To set the stage for reading as well as guide the reading process, skilled teachers encourage student use of graphic organizers such as K-W-L (Ogle, 1986) to help the students think about what they *K*now about the topic, what they *W*ant to know, and what they hope to *L*earn about the topic.

Effective teachers not only use prereading strategies, they also help students during reading. Their students will be asked to identify main concepts and details as they read by using concept maps, compare-contrast charts, or other graphic representations related to the text. These teachers may also read the selection aloud and model thinking about the text as they read. For example, by using a think-aloud (Jones and Seifert-Kessell, 1993), the teacher can assist the struggling reader with the process of thinking and assessing the text as he or she reads. This process guides comprehension and puts in place a model or strategy for the student to use when encountering difficult text.

Harvey and Goudvis (2000, p. 28) recommend several instructional strategies to help students construct meaning as they read. Teachers should model how they think about the passage as they read and share with their students how this strategy helps them to understand the meaning of the passage. Another important consideration is to connect this new strategy with the readers' prior knowledge. Helping the students connect the new strategy to other texts, genres, formats, disciplines, and contexts further enhances comprehension. Finally, the teacher should discuss the new strategy with the students and help them monitor their comprehension using the strategy.

Literacy Specialist/Literacy Coach
The role of the literacy specialist, or literacy coach, has become a valuable resource for struggling readers as well as for administrators and the teaching staff. This important individual understands literacy instruction, possesses leadership qualities, identifies assessments and analyzes results, and serves as a key figure for developing a high-quality secondary literacy initiative (Sturtevant, 2003).

Literacy intervention classes taught by the specialist should be offered in addition to the regular curriculum. If students are behind with literacy skills, they cannot easily catch up without specialized attention above and beyond the regular classroom teachers' use of instructional literacy strategies. Students need more time with reading and can receive the additional assistance in a class such as a reading elective taught by the specialist that allows for intensive one-on-one instruction. Intervention classes may be of short duration or require more time such as a semester-length program to help the student learn the deficient literacy skills. Intervention classes are not pull-outs, but additional time for the struggling reader to learn literacy skills required for success.

Freeport Intermediate School

Students at Freeport Intermediate School, Freeport, Texas, are hitting the ball out of the park when it comes to beating the opponents of low-level literacy and high-level poverty. Principal Clara Sale-Davis shared her school's successful plan to support the learning of all students by relationship-building and a common vision of high student performance. The high achieving school, located southwest of Houston, Texas, has a diverse population of 600 students, 54 percent Hispanic, 14 percent black, and 32 percent white. Sale-Davis also described the student population as highly mobile; the 25 percent mobility rate is due to high poverty and migrant status of the students' families. With these demographics, one would automatically assume that this school would be identified as struggling. However, the opposite is true. The school has moved from a 10 percent passage rate on the Texas Assessment of Knowledge and Skills (TAKS) to a 90 percent passage rate. When asked how this occurred, Sale-Davis shared a most revealing story of collaborative learning communities, assessment-driven instruction and learning, highly effective instructional strategies, and a school culture that is supportive of adult and student learning.

Profile

Freeport Intermediate School

1815 West 4th St. Freeport, TX 77651

Brazosport Independent School District

Principal: Clara Sale-Davis

- *600 students*
- *54 percent Hispanic, 14 percent black, 32 percent white*
- *70 percent free and reduced-price meals*
- *Recognitions: National Blue Ribbon School, Texas School of Excellence, NASSP Highly Successful Middle Level School*
- *National Forum to Accelerate Middle Level Reform School to Watch*

School Capacity and Collaborative Interactions Support Students

A school culture to support literacy for all began in 1992 when the school changed to a more flexible schedule organized around an A/B block concept. The schedule provided the framework to support interdisciplinary teams, professional learning communities, and, most important, student success. Sale-Davis shared a description of how this works at Freeport Intermediate School. There are four interdisciplinary teams: two teams of 150 students at each the seventh and eighth grades. There are 90 minute team planning sessions on "A days" so teachers can analyze student data and plan instruction based on content standards and identified student learning needs. "B days" provide vertical planning time for core content areas. This schedule provides time for professional learning opportunities, instructional planning, and creative interactions among the grade-level teams and departmental groups.

The school organization also includes five cadres that are organized around the five critical areas for school improvement. Each cadre includes stakeholders from every area of the school community: professional staff, support staff, students, and parents. *Planning and Communication Cadre* members plan the school calendar and specifically focus on planning for special events during the school year. Cadre members also ensure productive communication between school and home, school and community, and school and district. The *Staff Development Cadre* analyzes assessment data to identify the learning needs of students and teachers. The members then skillfully plan for the professional learning requirements of the teachers that will support the instructional program. The motto of the Staff Development Cadre is "If you don't go, you don't grow." The *School Climate Cadre* concentrates on the school climate and the morale of the staff. This team carefully analyzes discipline data, school climate issues, and classroom management practices. Understanding these data allows the plan to support a positive school climate for staff and students. The *Curriculum and Instruction Cadre* focuses on the master schedule, assessment, and the instructional program. The results of this cadre's planning efforts clearly encourage rigor and relevance of the curricula and are supportive of achievement for all. The *Assessment Cadre* intently analyzes multiple forms of assessment to understand the learning requirements of students and what instructional improvements are needed to support student learning. Data paint the canvas to understand the big picture of student and teacher learning needs.

The spirit of collaboration at Freeport is encouraged by the flexible schedule and the relationship-building within the teams and cadres. The block schedule provides the framework, but the relationships and team building actually grow from a common goal of excellence for staff and students. Sale-Davis passionately described how the staff grew in their understanding of student needs and began to let their creative juices coalesce around the need to support student achievement. One such example is the Elaboration Pageant held each year before the state writing assessment. Teachers have taught the writing process throughout the year, but the pageant provides a final focus that moves far beyond the traditional "drill and kill" worksheets prior to the test. Teachers, and even the administrator, take the primary roles of Allie Allusion, Minnie Metaphor, Sarah Simile, and Ella Elaboration. Using a beauty pageant format, the characters are given a prompt to which they respond. The bottom line is the need for Ella Elaboration to pull it all together so the original prompt becomes fully developed. This project grew from the collaboration, direction, and planning of the Language Arts Department. The students take the intended message from the pageant production, return to class, and participate in a final discussion of the value of elaboration techniques. As Sale-Davis described the activity, "It is 'drill and thrill' instead of 'drill and kill'."

Assessment Guides Instruction and Professional Development
Collaboration to support success begins with careful analysis of multiple forms of assessment. After focusing on curricula and instruction at the beginning of the school improvement process, test scores on TAKS improved dramatically; however, the reading scores still hovered at the 76th percentile mark. The Curriculum and Assessment Cadre carefully reviewed each target objective to determine areas for focus and improvement. The cadre determined the instructional teams were providing good support for teaching *some* critical literacy skills, but only 20 percent of the students were passing targets that measured making inferences, generalizations, and summarization.

The Curriculum and Instruction Cadre began to focus and plan to improve this identified deficit. First, the Language Arts Department defined "making inferences" for the entire staff. Then, collaboration began among all teams and departments to emphasize the critical skills for mastery. Sale-Davis gave an example of walking into a physical education class and hearing the teacher say, "Before we dress, let's summarize what we did today." The Math Department developed the "infamous hand," which became a symbol for summarization throughout the school. The fingers of the hand symbolized who, what, when, where, and how with a summary statement on the palm. Even the cheerleaders borrowed this graphic to advertise a school dance. At Freeport, assessment identified the need, but collaboration provided the direction for improvement.

There is a 20 percent turnover of teachers each academic year. Tongue-in-cheek, Sale-Davis said, "When you work in the 'hood, you just hope you have a teacher who can breathe." With the critical need for a highly effective teaching staff able to meet student-learning needs, the cadres zero in on what needs to be done to achieve success. For example, inclusion is an area of focus. To meet this goal, the school's culture is one of sharing and support. Paraprofessionals and striving teachers are paired with master teachers to facilitate the learning of best instructional strategies. The master teachers facilitate learning through shared teaching and planning. The new teachers observe these experts for 45 minutes of intensive instruction and student engagement. The observing teachers then have time to reflect on strategies and pedagogy used. They are later given the opportunity to question and interact with the master teacher. Prior to a formal observation by an administrator, the master teachers observe the striving teachers and provide substantive feedback related to practices. This collaboration builds such a level of collegial support that failure is not an option. In fact, Sale-Davis recently presented each teacher with a wristband for Valentine's Day that proudly boasts, "Failure Is Not an Option."

Instructional Practices Support Literacy for ALL

In both informal and formal classroom observations by the administration, the emphasis is on methodologies that engage students and facilitate learning for all. Intensive, well-defined instructional strategies support student literacy as teachers engage students with pre, during, and post learning/literacy strategies. These strategies activate students' prior knowledge and set a purpose for learning, as well as engage students with the topic through explicit reading and writing strategies. Students move beyond reading the text to critically thinking about, evaluating, and reflecting on the learning.

School Profile 4:
Freeport Intermediate School

Sale-Davis shared a recent observation of a science class to emphasize the pre, during, and post connections. The students were organized into learning teams, with the science teacher serving as facilitator. Students learned critical vocabulary prior to the lesson through a PowerPoint prelesson. The vocabulary was also creatively displayed on a vocabulary apron worn by the teacher to remind students of vocabulary as the class progressed. The heterogeneous team worked together with a packet of critical instructions and directions that were shared by the team reader. The students followed the directions in the chronological order required for a successful dissection. In one group, a special needs student successfully followed the directions to dissect the frog and label the parts as the group cooperatively worked together. This example is representative of instructional practices throughout the school that support academic rigor for all—struggling, striving, or gifted.

Success for ALL

Failure is not an option at Freeport Intermediate School, and this is clearly evident from the steps taken by the administration, staff, and community to support literacy for all. Multiple forms of student data provide the road map for attaining student improvement. If mastery of literacy skills is not achieved in the language arts class, students have an additional opportunity to participate in a skills support class during the last block of the school day. This time period provides the necessary structure for enrichment as well as reinforcement of critical literacy skills. Students needing additional support can receive specialized tutoring and one-on-one support provided in the computer lab. Lessons on the computer are prescriptive to address specific literacy needs of students, with a 45-minute follow-up and reinforcement by a teacher. The software disaggregates data to provide information related to benchmark attainment. If further support for student achievement is required, one form of intervention is an after-school tutorial. The mandatory tutorial is by invitation only; there is strong support from the parents and community—the local judge actually assigns students to the after-school tutoring in lieu of community service.

Freeport Reflects on Success of Staff and Students
Because of the students' impressive academic results, Freeport Intermediate has been recognized as a Blue Ribbon School by the U.S. Department of Education and as a School to Watch by the National Forum. Student success does not occur without commitment and laser-focused efforts to improve by the professional staff. The school culture at Freeport is intellectually stimulating and supportive of students across ethnic and socioeconomic groups. Success is due in part to Sale-Davis' visionary leadership; but, as she is quick to point out, the teaching staff continually strives for academic excellence of the students and professional excellence of the faculty. Expectations are high for continued academic success for all, and mediocrity is definitely not found in the vocabulary at Freeport Intermediate School.

6 Intervention: Meeting the Needs of ALL Students

As students enter middle and high school, most teachers assume that they arrive knowing how to read. However, the sad truth is that 25–35 percent of the students entering secondary-level grades have major deficits related to reading and comprehending grade-level texts. The dominant belief among both educators and the general public is that struggling students are not prepared to read from secondary textbooks because they do not have the foundation in phonics necessary to be an effective reader. And while in some instances this may be a reality, decoding problems for the adolescent are generally rare. The actual reading difficulties usually stem from a lack of comprehension strategies, inadequate vocabulary development, insufficient prior knowledge, poor reading fluency, and little or no motivation to read.

Educators often look for a simple "cookie-cutter" solution to solve literacy difficulties. As nice as it would be, a quick fix cannot be purchased at the local "education repair shop" or from the myriad companies touting their product as a cure-all for adolescent literacy ills. The reality is no product can substitute for a highly skilled teacher providing explicit instruction in all of the content areas and using research-based strategies embedded in the day-to-day instruction of course content. Additionally, adolescent readers, both at and below grade level, simply need more time to read during the school day.

Literacy is a complex, interactive, ongoing thinking process and requires a sophisticated approach to understanding text. To help struggling readers, teachers must help them learn the strategies that good readers use to extract meaning from text. Successful readers of all ages employ the following strategies:

- Use existing knowledge to make sense of new information

- Ask questions about the text before, during, and after reading

- Draw inferences from the text

- Monitor comprehension

- Use "fix-up" strategies when meaning breaks down

- Determine what is important

- Synthesize information to create new meaning (Pearson et al., 1992).

But what about the 2–5 percent of students reading two to three years below grade level? These students need immediate, intensive, accelerated instruction to improve reading deficits. Specialists trained in the use of intervention strategies and who understand the best approaches to teaching literacy should work with the struggling readers. This instruction should be assessment based and more intensive than the normal classroom program, and the students must be given additional time to learn and practice their literacy skills.

The ultimate goal throughout the process of intervention is to have all students reading and comprehending on grade level. Often the first thought on how to help a struggling reader is to send him or her to the reading teacher down the hall. Yet, this action has not proven successful in creating high-achieving readers. Struggling readers do need accelerated intensive instruction, but "yanking" them from a content class for literacy remediation is not the cure-all.

Schools wishing to create high-quality literacy experiences for their students must provide ample opportunities for readers at all levels to learn literacy strategies taught by highly skilled teachers. A successful literacy program will also stress the use of content-area interventions identified as being successful at helping both struggling and grade-level readers. Some of these interventions include using self-selected reading material, teaching skills of metacognition, activating prior knowledge, stressing the reading/writing connection, and using pre, during, and post literacy strategies.

Although an intervention plan is generally targeted at struggling readers, the literacy strategies included in this chapter are appropriate for *all* adolescent readers. Strategy instruction should be totally integrated into daily content instruction, as it is designed to encourage critical reading and thinking about text with a goal of student success for ALL.

Building an Intervention Program: Eight Actions Steps for the Literacy Leader

1. Develop an explicit schoolwide intervention plan.

If you truly want staff support for a schoolwide intervention plan, then all staff members need to be involved in developing the plan. A school should begin by working as grade-level and departmental teams to examine the data and determine a plan of action. The Alabama Reading Initiative (1999) suggests the following points of intervention to guide this planning:

- Explicit instruction in phonemic awareness

- Explicit instruction in phonics

- Direct and integrated instruction in text reading and comprehension

- Assessment-based selection and monitoring of struggling readers

- Accelerated, not decelerated, instruction

- More time for selected skills and strategies

- Intensive instruction in every session

- Extensive amounts of daily practice

- Teacher-directed instruction

- Finite time for duration of intervention

- Reduced teacher/pupil ratio

- Connections to classroom and parents

- Teachers who can deliver highly skilled instruction

- Continuously developing teachers of reading.

As an example, a school considering the above criteria could develop an action plan that includes:

- Interventions stated as measurable goal/objective(s)
- Steps or activities to meet the goal/objective(s)
- Person(s) responsible for completion of activity
- Additional resources needed
- Expected completion date
- Evidence to determine success
- Identification of who needs intervention.

The time spent on this endeavor will vary, based on student and school needs. The main idea behind exploring each of these 14 points is to identify your students' and school's needs and create a plan to address those identified as target areas. Each person at the school should play a significant role in developing the plan and be given a role in assuring that the goals/objectives are achieved.

To be successful, the plan must be continuously evaluated for progress and necessary changes made to the steps/activities when required. Another valuable aspect of this plan will be the generation of professional discussions among the staff. This will also assure that the plan does not become a document that sits on the shelf, and *success for all student readers* becomes the mantra for success.

2. Assign highly effective teachers to work with struggling readers.

A less-than-successful teacher is often assigned to teach an intervention class because it is thought the teacher may be more successful if he or she does not have a large number of students to teach. This is a major fallacy and is a disservice to our students. The most highly skilled teacher should be the one working with struggling readers. These are the teachers who have the knowledge of best strategies and know how to integrate them into their instructional plan. It is also critical that the teacher has an affinity with adolescent learners and can motivate them to want to read to learn. It is the principal's responsibility to assure that struggling students are taught by the best.

3. Create a balanced literacy intervention program.

A strong intervention program should be a combination of phonics instruction and whole language. Students should be given both specific, direct instruction of literacy skills and exposure to a wide array of literature and writing experiences. Depending on student need, research-based phonics programs may be a necessary addition to the secondary literacy program. These programs provide the intensive, explicit steps that are required to help students who need phonics instruction. It is especially important to provide balanced literacy instruction for the secondary struggling reader. They may need quick, intensive instruction with phonics skills, but it is critical that they also receive instruction in comprehension skills and literacy strategies.

4. Recruit volunteers to assist with the intervention program.

Volunteers can serve as an invaluable asset to a program by allowing teachers to focus their energies on direct service to students. However, it is important to research district and state guidelines for the use of volunteers; concerns for student privacy and security should be a major consideration. Guidelines must be set as to what activities volunteers may or may not help with.

If you use volunteers to listen to students read, provide them with training in the use of questioning skills and literacy strategies. Trained volunteers can be an invaluable help in a literacy improvement plan because they can guide students in the use of comprehension and metacognitive strategies as they read. However, even if the students are reading to an untrained volunteer, it can still be a worthwhile experience, as they are building automaticity and practicing their oral reading skills.

5. Develop a strong relationship with your feeder schools.

The ability to work with the staff of your feeder schools is essential if you wish to be ready to best serve the incoming students in the fall. Building this relationship is a critical element as you plan your school's intervention plan. In the spring, meet with your feeder elementary or middle schools to gather information about the incoming students' literacy levels and identified academic strengths/weaknesses. It is important to request all available assessment data on the incoming students because if the data are incomplete, it may be necessary to administer further diagnostic testing to have baseline data ready to use when the students enter.

This is a prime opportunity for teachers from the different schools to develop the vital link that should exist between schools within a district. This conversation and collaboration can not only provide information concerning the students' literacy levels, but can also strengthen the teaching of reading and writing across all grade levels.

6. Keep intervention classes small.

Research indicates that struggling students learn best when there is one-to-one or small-class instruction; therefore, as schedules are developed, consider how to keep the intervention classes small. This is often difficult because of budget constraints and lack of personnel, but to truly improve student literacy, it must happen. Teachers may be willing to take two to three more students in their class so that the literacy specialist can have smaller classes, or there may be opportunities for pairing intervention classes with periods of large class instruction such as band or physical education so that the regular classes will not be overloaded. There are multiple options, but the key is to creatively seek the best options for keeping the intervention class small.

7. Provide intensive, continuous professional development to help teachers become strategic teachers and students become strategic readers.

As was discussed in Chapter 4, professional development is key to any successful intervention plan. Teachers need to understand how students learn to read and how to diagnose reading difficulties. Recognizing that a student cannot read and comprehend at grade level is simple; knowing which strategy to use to help him or her develop meaning from text is more complex. The best way to diminish the number of students needing specialized intervention is to ensure that high-quality literacy instruction is occurring daily in *every* classroom.

What professional development is needed to improve students' literacy skills at your school? The answer becomes the basis for the literacy and professional development committees' planning for staff training. For example, students need to be able to use a wide variety of "fix-up" strategies when they do not understand what they are reading. Therefore, a key area of professional development is to provide teachers with the skills necessary to know what to teach (and how to teach it) in order to help students learn the required "fix-up" strategies.

Professional development should also be based on helping teachers understand which teaching strategies to incorporate within their daily instruction. Secondary teachers may be well-grounded in pedagogy of their subject, but understanding the best strategies for teaching literacy are not usually a major element of the college preparatory program for educators. Pressley (1998) concluded that despite 20 years of research on how to teach comprehension strategies, there was an alarming deficit of comprehension instruction in the classroom. The principal's role is to assure that comprehension instruction is occurring in every classroom and that teachers have the professional development necessary for them to deliver cognitive strategy instruction for all students.

Once the professional development has occurred, the principal can observe to verify if the teachers are using the instructional strategies in their day-to-day teaching and if they are modeling strategic literacy strategies so that students can begin to internalize the strategy and eventually use it on their own. The principal's presence in the classroom encourages teachers to use literacy strategies and ensure that the newly learned skills are being used to improve instruction. The National Reading Panel indicated that time and careful monitoring are required to assure that teachers and students are successful (National Reading Panel, 2000).

8. Use formative assessment data to guide every aspect of the intervention program.

The key to any successful intervention plan is ongoing or formative evaluation to determine if the program is working as planned. Encourage action research; it can be a vital form of assessment for teachers to evaluate the strategies they are using within their daily instruction. Data derived from action research can be a yardstick for defining the value of the action steps and help determine if changes need to be made.

Give teachers time to review data to understand the strengths and weaknesses of the action plan. Faculty meetings or time etched out of the schedule during the day will allow teachers time to examine the existing data and make any necessary changes to the action plan.

And Remember...

- As you consider purchasing a specific program to improve literacy, remember that highly skilled teachers are the key to student success, not a canned program that often ends up on the shelf after a year or so. Yes, teachers need materials, but even more, they need to learn more effective literacy and classroom instructional strategies.

- Do not rule out basic reading instruction in phonics. Secondary educators may question the use of phonemic awareness and phonics instruction, but there are generally some students in a school who need explicit instruction in this area. Special education students and some of the most deficient readers can benefit from help with basic word identification instruction and phonics.

- Keep your intervention balanced. Do not put all your eggs in one basket. Pull from a variety of sources to create an intervention plan that meets the needs of *your* students at your school. Very rarely does a program or plan work the same way in two different schools.

- Think outside the box. When faced with budget, personnel, or scheduling issues that negatively impact your intervention program, don't give up. Be creative, brainstorm with staff, talk with colleagues—something that someone else says may spark an idea that leads to a solution.

- Evaluate "canned" programs to ensure that research exists to support their effectiveness. Administrators are bombarded with materials purporting to be the answer to the literacy deficits of every struggling reader within the walls of the school. Speak with independent references at other schools where the program has been implemented.

Learn More About It: What the Experts and Research Say About Intervention Programs

The Alabama Reading Initiative (ARI) encourages participants in summer institutes to begin an intensive intervention program using research-based intervention strategies as early as possible in the child's educational program. These strategies should help to close the literacy deficit and should be consistently applied so that the intervention is short in duration (ARI, 1998). Successful literacy intervention programs are accelerated instead of decelerated (Allington, 2000; Davidson and Koppenhaver, 1993; Showers et al., 1998; Morris, Ervin, and Conrad, 1996). Allington (2000, p. 142), citing a study completed by Showers et al. (1998), recommended the following key tenets for a high school literacy intervention program:

- Reading appropriate books in school and at home

- Listening to teachers read good literature

- Instruction in active comprehension strategies

- Building vocabulary through reading

- Training in phonics and structural analysis

- Building vocabulary through natural language use.

Greenleaf et al. (2001) indicate many educators want to place struggling readers in remediation classes because of the rising numbers of high school students who do not read and comprehend on grade level. Yet, there is evidence that content-area teachers using explicit instructional strategies that focus on giving students effective comprehension strategies may be a better answer. And while the role of an *additional* (not pull-out) intensive intervention reading class continues to have a major role, the content-area teachers' value cannot be ignored.

There are several research reports or articles that stress successful strategies to build literacy in adolescent readers. Marlow Ediger (1997) believes students should have the opportunity to self-select their reading material because interest is a strong motivator and helps the reader to want to do more reading. The reading workshop model encouraged by Harvey and Goudvis (2000) also emphasizes self-selection of books. Vacca and Vacca (1999) encourage the use of questioning and brainstorming strategies, discussion, and other experientially based activities to help students focus on their own learning. Bryant et al. (1999) conclude that content reading instruction should be an important element of all secondary content curricula. The instructional plan should include opportunities for the student to learn strategies to identify new words and improve comprehension.

A successful intervention program will include ample opportunities for all students to be taught by highly skilled teachers using strategies that support learning. Effective strategies are multidimensional, utilizing multiple strategies, prior knowledge, and the students' metacognitive skills (Showers et al., 1998). Several content-area interventions that support effective literacy learning have been identified as successfully helping all students, regardless of their reading level.

Metacognition

In an interview with Lynn Olson, Walter Gibson (cited in Olson, 2001) indicates most students arriving in high school can decode text, but many have difficulty comprehending the text found in the textbooks. Abromitis (1994) indicates the most important goal of learning to read is comprehension, and she encourages the use of a strategy called metacognition, or thinking about thinking. Abromitis further stresses the importance of teachers assisting both proficient and struggling readers with thinking about the written text and processing the written word, which leads to comprehension. Lopez (1992) indicates metacognition involves students questioning themselves as they read the text and self-monitoring their understanding of the text. Students make sense of text when they are encouraged to think about what they read and how it relates to them personally (Greenleaf et al., 2001). Intervention strategies should involve training at-risk students to monitor their reading in order to become more metacognitively aware (Kamil et al., 2000). Campbell (1994) emphasizes the importance of teachers modeling metacognitive strategies. This instruction should include:

- Helping students to make connections between new information and prior knowledge by using the written text as the foundation

- Discussing the events in the story in order to make a connection with the student's own experiences

- Participating in discussions that include higher-order-thinking questions related to the text.

Activating Prior Knowledge

Another strategy that effective readers use to comprehend text is activating prior knowledge. Ausubel (1968) indicates that one of the most important criteria for a student to comprehend text involves stimulating what he or she already knows. Schema experts theorize that learners use prior knowledge to better understand new text. Prior knowledge is schema, or a pattern of knowledge that is formed from prior experiences. It is an important mental use of schemata to find meaning or comprehension in text (Carey, Harste, and Smith, 1977; Pressley et al., 1990). Hennings (1994, as cited in Manzo, 2001) indicates that students better understand what they read when they make a connection between the text and their prior knowledge (p. 16). Berger and Robinson (1982) stress that prior knowledge must be activated or reading comprehension cannot occur. Students learn to use or activate prior knowledge as the basis for all learning (Vacca and Vacca 1999). Harniss et al. (2001) stress the importance of teachers actively engaging the students' background knowledge by first determining their specific learning needs and then teaching information they need in order to understand the material that will be contained in the text of the lesson.

Balanced Approach

Research dating back to 1967 indicates the best approach to teaching literacy is a balanced approach—a combination of whole language and phonics instruction (Bond and Dykstra, 1967). Adams (1990) says all children, particularly at-risk readers, should be exposed to a rich variety of reading and writing experiences as well as explicit, direct instruction. Although the phonics–whole language debate focuses on elementary students, literacy instruction should continue in middle school and high school, and current research indicates that effective secondary literacy instruction is multidimensional and should focus on more than one element of the literacy process (Showers et al., 1998). An IRA (1999) position statement emphatically states, "Literacy development of adolescents is just as important and requires just as much attention as that of beginning readers" (p. 1).

The Reading/Writing Connection

Researchers have discovered a definite link between reading and writing, and during the past decade there has been a greater emphasis on helping secondary students use the reading/writing connection to learn more information and to use higher-order-thinking skills in the various content areas (Tierney and Pearson, 1992; Alvermann and Moore, 1991). Moje, Dillon, and O'Brien (2000, p. 165) found in their study that "learning in the secondary disciplines—or content areas—is shaped by the reading and writing that learners do in those disciplines." Writing activities integrated into all subject areas help students make meaningful connections to the text read. Writing activities should include essays and reports, descriptions of events, journal entries, written explanations of science procedures, and written explanations for solving a math problem (Misulis, 2000).

Pre, During, and After Reading Strategies

Reading comprehension involves the act of thinking and making meaning before, during, and after reading by connecting the information being read with the reader's prior knowledge (Snider, 1989). Effective readers use strategies to develop comprehension that involve (a) knowing the reason or purpose for reading, (b) identifying the difference between significant and less important information within the text, (c) questioning oneself about the text as it is being read, and (d) identifying and correcting any comprehension problems as they occur during reading (Bryant et al., 1999, p. 297). Graphic organizers assist readers with organizing and comprehending difficult passages such as expository text (Brigham, Scruggs, and Mastropieri, 1995).

Buckhorn High School

Buckhorn High School in New Market, AL, exemplifies what can occur when a school makes 100 percent literacy its goal and implements the changes that ensure its eventual achievement. A collaborative effort of administration, faculty, and other key individuals began the process to develop a culture of literacy in 1999 when the school was selected by the Alabama State Department of Education to participate in the Alabama Reading Initiative Summer Academy and to serve as a Literacy Demonstration Site. Buckhorn is located in the middle of former cotton fields just outside of Huntsville, AL. The demographics and student population began to change dramatically more than 10 years ago as new families moved into the community from the larger neighboring city, and the children of migrant workers, who spoke very limited English, began to swell the student rolls.

Principal Tommy Ledbetter described his school as an average school 10 years ago, but he stressed two factors that have changed Buckhorn from an average to an award-winning school. These factors include conversion to a block schedule and participation in the Alabama Reading Initiative (ARI). ARI is a comprehensive and systemic reading improvement system sponsored by the Alabama State Department of Education. In 1998, Buckhorn students' reading scores on the Stanford Achievement Test were the lowest scores on the school's total test battery. This fact motivated the staff to commit to two weeks of intensive literacy training and to begin a change of traditional instructional strategies. The block schedule also provided more opportunities for creative scheduling to meet the needs of students and options for changing from traditional lectures to more creative teaching strategies.

Leadership Is Key to Achieving Literacy Goals

Strong leadership is an essential building block to constructing a successful literacy program and seems to be firmly established at Buckhorn. Administrators and the literacy leadership team at Buckhorn are committed to improving classroom instruction; developing professional learning communities; analyzing assessment to guide instruction and professional development; and developing intensive intervention strategies to meet the literacy needs of students reading two to three grade levels below their current grade level. Ledbetter said, "I had to become totally involved, and the faculty knew that I was committed 100 percent to focusing on literacy at our school." He stressed that his philosophy related to reading instruction totally changed: "I used to think we assigned reading, but I now firmly believe that we teach reading."

Ledbetter stressed that his role is to provide the teachers with every available resource to achieve the school goal of 100 percent literacy. This role often requires him to seek financial resources, analyze test data, provide time during the day for ongoing professional learning and planning, and encourage teacher excellence through collegial classroom visits. According to Ledbetter, data must drive professional development and school improvement efforts; therefore, he, along with the literacy leadership team, carefully analyzes data to determine the instructional needs of students and professional development requirements for teachers. Reliance on the findings and

Profile

Buckhorn High School

4123 Winchester Road
New Market, AL 35761

Principal:
Tommy Ledbetter

- *925 students*
- *26 percent minority*
- *10 percent free and reduced-price meals*
- *96 percent graduation rate*
- *Recognitions: U.S. Department of Education Blue Ribbon High School, 2002*

recommendations of the school literacy team prompts him to explore all avenues of funding to support the literacy program. Indicating that no source of funding has been left unexplored, Ledbetter said donations, grants, general funds, and discretionary funds have been combined to purchase books for the library and classrooms; fund ongoing professional development; and acquire additional test protocols. He says, "Our number one priority is literacy, and I'll find the money to support it."

To fully implement innovative programs a philosophical change often must occur. The philosophical shift in Buckhorn administrators' thinking is evident in their enthusiastic support of a secondary literacy program and their understanding that personalizing the educational plan for each student is critical to success. Ledbetter stated, "I want our faculty to know, and they do, that reading drives everything we do. It goes across all content areas." Sarah Fanning, Buckhorn's instructional administrator, indicates, "We have become a more compassionate school because we consider each student special, and we truly plan for each student's success."

Assessment Guides Decision Making

Assessment plays a vital role in implementing Buckhorn's literacy program, according to Ledbetter. Multiple assessments are carefully analyzed and used to determine the direction of the school's literacy improvement plan. After carefully analyzing data in 1998, the faculty and administration discovered that 225 of the 331 ninth and tenth grade students at Buckhorn were reading and comprehending below grade level. Fanning said, "I was shocked. I could not sleep for days when I saw the number of students who were reading below grade level." According to Fanning, it was a life-changing experience to know that those students were walking the hallways of the high school and were reading on a fourth and fifth grade level. Their mission became to understand the student needs and develop a plan to address the problem.

Every decision that is made at Buckhorn is based on identified student and teacher needs. Originally, data from the Stanford Achievement Test were used to identify struggling readers, but the data now include results from other assessments, such as Woodcock Reading Mastery. As new ninth graders enter Buckhorn, staff members look at the Stanford results as a baseline to understand where students are and then determine if additional assessments are required to more fully reveal specific student literacy strengths and weaknesses. Then, an action plan is developed to address student literacy needs.

Ledbetter indicated that the school assessment committee meets regularly to analyze student assessments and then develop a comprehensive plan to address identified needs. Every content area teacher develops student profiles and an action plan for improvement of instruction to meet student needs.

Improved literacy opportunities for all students at Buckhorn have helped students to achieve 100 percent passage rate for the past few years on the Alabama High School Graduation Exam, which tests students' mastery of content standards in math, English, history, and science. In addition, the dropout rate has decreased. On the surface, Buckhorn's dropout rate appears high since migrant students enter ninth grade at Buckhorn, but move away in October of their freshman year to Florida and do not return as sophomores the following year. If this factor is removed from the equation, the dropout rate has decreased from 5.4 percent to 3.2 percent.

Professional Development a Necessary Ingredient

Teachers began the process of adding literacy strategies to their daily instruction after attending the two-week ARI Summer Reading Academy. They learned research-based literacy strategies, but they soon discovered the foundation of a few core literacy strategies were not enough. Instead, ongoing professional development has been the key to assisting the teachers with the skills to fully integrate literacy strategies into their daily instructional plan. Teachers plan together and use action research to determine actual strategies that work with their students.

Every professional learning activity is based on data that indicate student and teacher needs, which Ledbetter feels is important because teacher performance in the classroom is the key. He gave an example of current history teachers, who are all new to the classroom. Their primary need is professional development to learn literacy strategies that work in their classrooms. The literacy coach works with new teachers and models research-based strategies in the classroom. Shared teaching experiences help teachers to work with one another to practice strategies, analyze effectiveness, and improve instruction.

Strategic Teaching Makes a Difference

School Profile 5:
Buckhorn High School

Administrators and teachers at Buckhorn articulated that their attitudes toward teaching reading at the secondary level have changed. Fanning said before adopting their literacy initiative, teachers saw themselves as individuals and isolated, working to achieve academic goals within their personal classrooms. That view has transformed to seeing themselves as part of a collaborative team focused on student and teacher needs. "We now realize that we are a team that can achieve if we put our talents together," said Fanning. Part of the process was to dissect the curriculum. "We refocused everything we were doing from an instructional standpoint," Ledbetter said. Administrators and teachers work together to identify common goals, develop action plans, and prescribe needed professional development. Both Fanning and Ledbetter shared how they had changed from monitoring to being actively involved with teams of teachers and committees.

Teachers throughout the building provided insight into how they viewed their roles after committing to a literacy program. A science teacher said, "I feel I must find specific strategies to help my students read and comprehend text if I am really doing my job." Another teacher said, "I've come to understand that reading instruction with specific comprehension strategies really makes a difference, especially in high school. It's my job to see that it happens."

Pulling It Together

Administrators and teachers at Buckhorn continue to evaluate student data and teacher professional learning needs to determine the direction of the literacy program. The addition of a ninth and tenth grade reading/language elective has provided additional support for students reading significantly below their current grade level. Content teachers have become strategic teachers and help students to make critical connections to text with pre, during, and post reading strategies. Student performance at Buckhorn continues to improve. Has the goal of 100 percent literacy been achieved? No, but the framework is in place, and the staff continue to seek opportunities to improve learning opportunities for all students.

of the room, she found it very difficult to engage the stairs, as intended until towards

7 Final Thoughts

A secondary-literacy specialist for middle and high schools remarked on the fact that different schools were responding very differently to the literacy training she was providing. When asked what made the difference in her success, she responded: "The principal."

In schools with a leader who demonstrated his or her support by being present during the training and taking part in the discussions, the school was much more likely to embrace the work and make literacy instruction part of its daily practice. On the other hand, in schools where the principal had merely introduced her and walked out of the room, she found it very difficult to engage the staff, as they did not perceive literacy training as a valuable use of their time.

The role of today's principal is so vast and complex that the thought of adding one more thing to the mix can seem daunting. A principal is expected to be an instructional leader, a facilities manager, a budget analyst, a personnel supervisor, a creative problem-solver, a student disciplinarian—the list goes on and on. Why, then, should today's secondary principals place a priority on becoming literacy leaders for their schools? The statistics on adolescent literacy contained in this *Leader's Guide* spell out the answer. Far too many of our middle school and high school students are unable to read at the level necessary to achieve academic success in the content areas. Students who leave our schools without the necessary literacy skills face an uncertain future; they are at risk for causing disruptive behavior, for dropping out, or for participating in risky behaviors that endanger their health or future success.

As principals, we must take on the challenge of becoming the literacy leaders in our schools simply because it is our responsibility to do so; in the words of Michael Fullan (2003), it is "the moral imperative of the principal (to lead) deep cultural change that mobilizes the passion and commitment of teachers, parents, and others to improve the learning of all students, including closing the achievement gap." If we wish to close the achievement gap, then we must tackle the literacy issue in our individual schools.

As you ponder how best to use this guide to improve literacy efforts at your school, remember Stephen Covey's principle for success—*begin with the end in mind*.

Change begins with a vision—a vision that grows out of the mind of the school leader and into the heart of others. So take a few moments to imagine your school as it might appear with a fully functional literacy plan in place. Visits to classrooms would find students actively engaging in the learning, holding in-depth conversations regarding the concepts being learned, and using literacy strategies to comprehend and analyze texts. Listening to teacher conversations in the lunchroom or during team meetings would reveal dialogue on literacy strategies that have been successfully implemented and discussions about how best to help a student achieve success across the content areas. Looking around, you would see hallways filled with posters and displays supporting literacy, and classrooms filled with literary resources. At first glance, it would be easy to mistake a science or health class for a language arts class, as the teacher would use pre-reading strategies to introduce a lesson. Students who struggle despite the literacy-rich environment would be given opportunities for additional help and support that would enable them to improve their reading skills. As you picture this scenario in your school, you may see many pieces already in place, but you also may realize some pieces of the puzzle are still missing.

What is the secret to literacy success for your school? Make changes one step at a time. This book contains a wealth of ideas for principals who are seeking to improve the literacy efforts of their schools. Those of you reading this have two choices: put it on the shelf, or begin to act upon it. To quote another principle from Covey—*put first things first*. Decide what you can change and what changes will have the most impact on the greatest number of students. Implementing the program outlined in this guide will not be easy, nor will it happen quickly. In 1999, the International Reading Association published a position paper on adolescent literacy that states, "Literacy development is an ongoing process, and it requires just as much attention for adolescents as it does for beginning readers. In today's fast-paced world, literacy demands are expanding, and they include more reading and writing tasks than at any other time in history. Adolescents need high levels of literacy to understand the vast amount of information available to them, and to fuel their imaginations as they help create the world of the future."

Our students deserve school leaders who understand the importance of literacy and who strive to prepare *all* students to meet the challenges they will face in the future. For every day we put off giving literacy issues the attention they deserve, more students fall further and further behind. As principal, you are the key to literacy success at your school. Begin the journey today.

References

Abromitis, B. (1994). *The role of metacognition in reading comprehension: Implications for instruction.* (Literacy Research Report No. 19) Northern Illinois Univ., Dekalb MI: Curriculum and Instruction Reading Clinic. (ERIC Document Reproduction Service No. ED371291).

Adams, M. J. (1990). *Beginning to read: Thinking and learning about print.* Cambridge, MA: MIT Press.

Alabama Reading Initiative. (2003). *Secondary training manual.* ALSDE: Montgomery, AL.

Alabama Reading Initiative. (2004). *Literacy coach training manual.* ALSDE: Montgomery, AL.

Alabama Reading Panel. (1998). *Report of the review of the research.* (Available from: The Alabama State Department of Education, Gordon Persons Building, 50 North Ripley Street, Montgomery, AL 36130).

Alliance for Excellent Education. (2003). *Adolescents in crisis.* Paper presented at the first annual American High School Policy Conference. Washington, DC.

Allington, R. L. (2000). *What really matters for struggling readers: Designing research-based programs.* New York: Longman.

Alvermann, D. E., & Moore, D. W. (1991). Secondary school reading. In R. Barr, M.L. Kamil, P.B. Mosenthal, & P. D. Pearson (Eds.), *Handbook of reading research: Vol. II.* New York: Longman.

Anderson, R., Wilson, P., & Fielding, L. (1988). Growth in reading: How children spend their time outside of school. *Reading Research Quarterly, 3.*

Ausubel, D. P. (1968). *Educational psychology: A cognitive view.* New York: Holt, Rinehart and Winston.

Biancarosa, G., & Snow, C. E. (2004) *Reading next—A vision for action and research in middle and high school literacy: A report from Carnegie corporation. of New York.* Washington, DC: Alliance for Excellent Education, 12.

Berger, A., & Robinson, H. A. (1982). *Secondary school reading: What research reveals for classroom practice.* Urbana, IL: ERIC Clearinghouse on Reading and Communication Skills.

Bond, G. L., & Dykstra, R. (1967). The cooperative research program in first-grade reading instruction. *Reading Research Quarterly, 2,* 5–142.

Bradley, D. H. (1998). Addressing school reform: What's essential and what's not. *Reading Today, 16,* 18–20. Retrieved July 22, 2001 from http://www.mhsl.uab.edu: 2080/ehost.asp?key=204.179.122.130_8000_1485596322&site=ehost&return=n& profile=web.

Brigham, F. J., Scruggs, T. E., & Mastropieri, M. A. (1995). Elaborative maps for enhanced learning of historical information: Uniting spatial, verbal, and imaginal information. *The Journal of Special Education, 28,* 440–460. (Cited in Bryant, D., Ugel, N., Thompson, S., & Hamff, A., 1999.)

Bryant, D., Ugel, N., Thompson, S., & Hamff, A. (1999). Instructional strategies for content-area reading instruction. *Intervention in school & clinic, 34(5),* 293–305. Retrieved July 14, 2001 from http://www.mhsl.uab.edu:2305/ehost .asp?key= 204.179.122.129_8000_-953479593&site=ehost&return=n&profile=web.

California Dept. of Education. (1996). *Teaching reading: A balanced comprehensive approach to teaching reading in pre-kindergarten through grade three.* Sacramento, CA: California Department of Education.

Campbell, T. K. (1994). *Becoming autonomous: What research suggests and how autonomy can be facilitated in secondary reading programs.* Paper presented at the Annual Meeting of the College Reading Association (38th) New Orleans, LA. November 3–6, 1994. (ERIC Document Reproduction Service No. ED379650).

Carey, R. F., Harste, J. C., & Smith, S. L. (1981). Contextual constraints and discourse processes: A replication study. *Reading Research Quarterly. 12(2),* 201–212. (ERIC Document Reproduction Service No. EJ 240 348).

Children's Literacy Network. (2001). *A blueprint for literacy leadership: The principal's role in improving literacy instruction.* Retrieved from http://www.cliontheweb.org/ principals_blueprint.html

Darling-Hammond, L. (1997). What matters most: 21st-century teaching. *Education Digest, 6(3),* 4–10.

Davidson, J., & Koppenhaver, D. (1993). *Adolescent literacy: What works and why* (2nd ed.). Hamden, CT: Garland.

Donahue, P. L., Voehl, K. E., Campbell, J. R., & Mazzeo, D. (1999) *Reading report card executive summary.* Retrieved from: http://nces.ed.gov/nationsreport/pubs/ main.1998/1999500.shtml.1999.

Ediger, M. (1997). Transescents, classroom interaction and reading. *Reading Improvement, 34,* 176–181.

Fullan, M. (2003). *The moral imperative of school leadership.* Thousand Oaks, CA: Corwin.

Frey, M., Zipperer, M., Worley, T., Sisson, M., & Said, R. (2002). *Literacy education and reading programs in the secondary school: Status, problems, and solutions.* NASSP Bulletin. *(86) 632,* 3–18.

Gaskins, I. (1998). There's more to teaching at-risk and delayed readers than good reading instruction. In Padak, N., Rasinski, T., Peck, J., Church, B., Fawcett, G., Hendershot, J., Henry, J. et al. (Eds.). *Distinguished educators on reading* (1st ed., pp. 209–224). Newark, Delaware: International Reading Association.

Gassenheimer, K. (Summer, 2003). *How "powerful conversations" began.* Working Toward Excellence, The Journal Of The Alabama Best Practices Center. Montgomery, AL: Best Practices Center vol. 3: 3, 4–5.

Gibbons, S., & Kimmell, H. (1997). Changing teacher behavior through staff development: Implementing the teaching and content. *School Science & Mathematics, 97(6),* 302–400.

Greenleaf, C., Schoenback, R., Cziko, C., & Mueller, F. (2001). Apprenticing adolescent readers to academic literacy. *Harvard Educational Review,* 79–129. Retrieved June 27, 2001, from http://www.gse.harvard.edu/~hepg/p01.htm#green

Harniss, M., Dickson, S., Kinder, D., & Hollenbeck, K. (2001). Textual problems and instructional solutions: Strategies for enhancing learning from published history textbooks. *Reading & Writing Quarterly, 17,* 127–150.

Harvey, S., & Goudvis, A. (2000). *Strategies that work.* New York: Stenhouse.

International Reading Association. (1999). *Summary of adolescent literacy: A position statement for the commission on adolescent literacy of the international reading association.* International Reading Association, Inc.: Washington, DC.

International Reading Association. (1998). *Roles for reading specialists.* International Reading Association, Inc.: Washington, DC.

Jones, L., & Seifert-Kessell, N. (1993). Using think alouds to enhance children's comprehension monitoring abilities. *The Reading Teacher* 47(3).

Kamil, M., Mosenthal, P., Pearson, P. D., & Barr, R. (2000). *Handbook of reading research (Vol. III).* Mahwah, NJ: Lawren Erlbaum Assoc.

Kelleher, J. (June 2003). *A model for assessment-driven professional development.* Phi Delta Kappan, 00317217, vol. 84, 10.

King, M. B., & Newmann, F. M. (2000). Will teacher learning advance school goals? *Phi Delta Kappan* 81 i8576. Retrieved August 8, 2001 from http://www.mhsl.uab.edu:2305/ehost.asp?key=204.179.122.129_8000_-953479593&site=ehost&return=n&profile=web

Learning First Alliance. (1998). *Every child reading: An action plan of the Learning First Alliance.* Retrieved July 8, 2001 from http://www.readbygrade3.com/lfa.htm.

Leithwood, K., Louis, K., Anderson, S., & Wahlstron, K. (2004). *Review of how leadership influences student learning.* A Report for the Wallace Foundation. Retrieved March 8, 2005 from http://www.wallacefoundation.org/NR/rdonlyres/E3BCCFA5-A88B-45D3-8E27-B973732283C9/0/ReviewofResearchLearningFromLeadership.pdf.

Lopez, P. (1992). *Metacognitive strategies for teaching reading to elementary students.* (ERIC Document Reproduction Service No. ED348650).

Manzo, K. (2001). A primary subject goes secondary. *Education Week,* 20(31), 13–17. Retrieved June 24, 2001, from http://www.sasked.gov.sk.ca/docs/mls/read.html.

MacDonald, I. (2001). The teaching community: recreating university teaching. *Teaching in Higher Education, 6(2),* 153–168. Retrieved July 12, 2001 from http://www.mhsl.uab.edu:2080/ehost.asp?key=204.179.122.129_8000_462389588&site=ehost&return=n&profile=web.

Misulis, K. (2000). Literacy 2000. *Contemporary Education.* 71(3), 17–21. Retrieved July 14, 2001 from http://www.mhsl.uab.edu.

Moje, E., Dillon, D., & O'Brien, D. (Jan/Feb 2000). Reexamining roles of learner, text, and context in secondary literacy. *Journal of Educational Research.* 93(3), 165–181. Retrieved January 27, 2001, from http://www.mhsl.uab.edu/ebscohost.fulltext.asp?resultSetId=R00000002&hitNum=3&booleanTerm=AU%20%22Moje%20.

Morris, D., Ervin, C., & Conrad, K. (1996). A case study of middle school reading disability. *Reading Teacher, 49.* 368–377.

National Staff Development Council. (2001). *Standards for staff development.* Oxford, OH: NSDC.

National Association of Secondary School Principals. (2004). *Breaking ranks II: Strategies for leading high school reform.* NASSP: Reston, VA. 23.

National Reading Panel. (2000). *Report of the National Reading Panel: Teaching children to read: An evidence-based assessment of the scientific research literature on reading and its implications for reading instruction* (Reports of the subgroups). Rockville, MD: National Institute of Child Health and Human Development.

National Center for Educational Statistics. (2001). *National NAEP results.* Washington, DC: Retrieved online from http://nces.ed.gov/programs/coe/2001/charts.

Norton, J. (Summer, 2003). *Powerful conversations can transform teacher learning.* Working Toward Excellence: The Journal of The Alabama Best Practices Center. Montgomery, AL: Best Practices Center, vol 3, 3. (1–2).

Ogle, D. M. (1986). K-W-L: A teaching model that develops active reading in expository text. *The Reading Teacher,* 39(6). 564–570.

Olson, L. (2001). A quiet crisis: Unprepared for high stakes. *Education Week on the Web.* Retrieved August 5, 2001, from http://www.edweek.org/ew/ewstory.cfm?slug=31catchup.h20.

Pearson, P. D., Roehler, L., Dole, J., & Duffy, G. (1992). Developing expertise in reading comprehension. In J. Samuels and A. Farstrup (Eds.), *What Research Has to Say About Reading Instruction*: Newark, DE: International Reading Association.

Pennell, J. R., & Firestone, W. A. (1998). Teacher-to-teacher professional development through state-sponsored networks. *Phi Delta Kappan,* 79(5), 354–357. Retrieved July 13, 2001, from http://www.mhsl.uab.edu:2079/ehost.asp?key=204.179.122.130_8000_173 1493105&site=ehost&return=n&profile=web.

Phillips, M. P. (2002). *Secondary teacher perceptions relating to Alabama Reading Initiative training and implementation.* (Doctoral dissertation, University of Alabama & University of Alabama in Birmingham, Birmingham, Alabama).

Pressley, M. (1998). *Reading instruction that works: The case for balanced teaching.* New York: Guilford.

Pressley, M., Woloshyn, V., Lysynchuk, L., & Martin, V. (1990). A primer of research on cognitive strategy instruction: The important issues and how to address them. *Educational Psychology Review, 2*(1), 1–58.

Raiche, N. (2000). A second chance to learn to read. *Leadership, 30*(2), 18–20.

RAND Reading Study Group. (2002). *Reading for understanding: Toward a research and development program in reading comprehension.* Santa Monica, CA: RAND Corporation.

Reys, B. J., Reys, R. E., Barnes, D., Beem, J., & Papick, I. (1997). Collaborative curriculum investigation as a vehicle for teacher enhancement and mathematics curriculum reform. *School Science and Mathematics, 97.* 253–259.

Schon, D. A. (1988). Educating the reflective teaching. In P. P. Grimmett & G. E. Erickson (Eds.), *Reflection in teacher education.* New York: Teachers College Press. 19–30.

Showers, B., Joyce, B., Scanlon, M., & Schnaubelt, C. (1998). A second chance to learn to read. *Educational Leadership, 55*(6), 27–30.

Snider, V. E. (1989). Reading comprehension performance of adolescents with learning disabilities. *Learning Disability Quarterly, 12,* 87–96.

Sparks, D. & Hirsh, S. (1997). *A new vision for staff development.* Alexandria, VA: Association for Supervision and Curriculum.

Strickland, D. (2004). *Improving reading achievement through professional development.* Rutgers University.

Sturtevant, E. (2003). *The literacy coach: A key to improving teaching and learning in secondary schools.* Alliance for Excellent Education: Washington, DC.

Tierney, R. J., & Pearson, P. D. (1992). Learning to learn from text: A framework for improving classroom practice. In E.K. Dishner, T.W. Bean, J.E. Readence & D. W. Moore (Eds.), *Reading in the content areas: Improving classroom instruction* (pp. 87–103). Dubuque, IA: Kendall/Hunt.

Vacca, R. T., & Vacca, J. L. (1999). *Content area reading* (6th ed.) New York, NY: Longman.

Wenglinsky, H. (2001). How teaching matters: Bringing the classroom back into discussions of teacher quality. *Educational Testing Service Monograph.* As cited in *T H E Journal.* (June 2001). V28 i11 p. 12. Retrieved August 8, 2001, from http://www.mhsl.uab.edu:2305/ehost.asp?key=204.179.122.129_8000_530496918&site=ehost&return=n&profile=web.

Wiggins, G. (1997). Work standards: Why we need standards for instructional and assessment design. *NASSP Bulletin* 81(590). 56–64.

Appendix 1:
Annotated Bibliography
of Literacy Resources

Adolescent Literacy Across the Curriculum

Alvermann, D. E. (2002, Summer). Effective literacy instruction for adolescents. *Journal of Literacy Research* 34(2), 189–208. (ERIC Document Reproduction Service No. EJ672862).

Discusses the importance of keeping adolescents' interests and needs foremost in mind when designing literacy instruction at the middle and high school level. Argues that effective adolescent literacy instruction must address issues of self-efficacy and student engagement with a variety of texts in diverse settings. Contends that literacy instruction must also attend to literacy demands of subject-area classes, struggling readers, issues of critical literacy, and to participatory instructional approaches.

Avery, C. W. and others. (1996, November). On the road to school reform: Mapping a route into secondary reading programs. *Journal of Adolescent & Adult Literacy* 40(3), 214–16. (ERIC Document Reproduction Service No. EJ542540).

Describes a successful schoolwide reading program at one high school, which sought to change students' attitudes toward reading. Discusses envisioning the program, promoting it, gathering momentum, and ensuring its continued success.

Blokker, B., Simpson, A., and Whittier, P. (2002, Spring). Schoolwide literacy: The principal's role. Leading literacy communities. *Middle Matters* 7.

Emphasizes the importance of middle level principals making literacy a schoolwide issue. Principals need to create and maintain a schoolwide reading culture because students are transitional readers who vary in their ability to read and understand what they read.

Brozo, W.G., and Hargis, C. (2003, September). Taking seriously the idea of reform: One high school's efforts to make reading more responsive to all students. *Journal of Adolescent & Adult Literacy* 47(1), 14–23.

Describes how subject-area teachers at one high school used grant money to change their teaching styles, significantly improving students' reading abilities. Details how reading achievement testing was conducted and the results were translated into effective literacy reforms designed to go beyond "teaching to the middle." Tracks the experiences of two students at either end of the reading ability continuum and the effects the initiatives had on them.

Fenn, J. (2005, February). Eight ways your librarian can help promote literacy. *Principal Leadership* 5(6), 49–51.

These practical suggestions enable the school librarian to play a central role in promoting and developing student literacy.

Fisher, D. (2001, October). "We're moving on up": Creating a schoolwide literacy effort in an urban high school. *Journal of Adolescent & Adult Literacy* 45(2), 92–101. (ERIC Document Reproduction Service No. EJ632349).

Presents an example of how professional development measures and an integrated approach to literacy positively affected one urban high school. Notes that the reading achievement of these urban high school youths was influenced by quality instruction and support for classroom teachers. Indicates that school structures influence student achievement.

Grady, K. (2002, December). Adolescent literacy and content area reading. *ERIC Digest.* (ERIC Document Reproduction Service No. ED469930).

Noting a renewed interest in and dedication to the rights and needs of adolescent readers, this digest addresses the development of content-area reading, discusses recent reconceptualizations of the field, and offers a new model for classroom practice. It begins with a brief description of the historical context of literacy development in the secondary grades, focusing on developments in cognitive psychology in the 1970s and 1980s, and more recent efforts to move away from viewing reading solely as a cognitive process. The digest then discusses recent efforts to conceptualize the reading process as including a social dimension, literacy practices beyond the classroom, an expanded notion of text, and the relationship between literacy and identity. It concludes with a description of the Reading Apprenticeship model, an instructional framework based on the dual notions of literacy as a complex cognitive and social process and of teaching as cognitive apprenticeship.

Massey, D. D., and Heafner, T. L. (2004, September). Promoting reading comprehension in social studies. *Journal of Adolescent & Adult Literacy* 48(1), 26–40.

Researchers suggest there is a reading crisis in middle and secondary schools. However, many content-area teachers do not consider themselves reading teachers, nor do they know how to help students develop comprehension skills. Using the Scaffolded Reading Experience approach as a framework, this article provides content-area teachers with concrete techniques for teaching reading and content through textbook, primary, and fictional sources.

Meltzer, J. (2002). *Adolescent Literacy Resources: Linking Research and Practice.* (ERIC Document Reproduction Service No. ED466788).

Secondary school educators too often find that their students do not have the necessary literacy skills to use reading and writing effectively to learn subject matter. For middle and high school educators searching for ways to promote literacy, this book bridges the divide between what the research says works in literacy and what is happening in most of today's content-area classrooms. The book reviews relevant research from the past 20 years and describes the implications for classroom practice. The first section of the book provides an overview of the issues related to ongoing adolescent literacy support and development, followed by an introduction to the Adolescent Literacy Support Framework. Each of the next four sections are devoted to one of the key components of the framework. Each section contains a summary of the research for that key component, followed by annotated reviews of resources that provide insights into the implications of the research and illustrate implementation of research-based practices. The extensive bibliography includes all of the citations found in the book as well as many more studies and resources of value to educators interested in learning more. The book is divided into the following sections: Introduction; The Adolescent Literacy Support Framework; Overview of Key Component A: Address Student Motivation to Read and Write; Overview of Key Component B: Implement Research-Based Literacy Strategies for Teaching and Learning; Overview of Key Component C: Integrate Reading and Writing across the Curriculum; and Overview of Key Component D: Ensure Support, Sustainability, and Focus through Organizational Structures and Leadership Capacity.

Meltzer, J. (2001). Supporting adolescent literacy across the content areas. *Perspectives on Policy and Practice* (ERIC Document Reproduction Service No. ED459442).

Literacy—the ability to read, write, speak, listen, and think effectively— enables adolescents to learn and to communicate clearly in and out of school. Adolescents need to have strong literacy skills so that they can understand academic content, communicate in a credible way, participate in cultural communities, and negotiate the world. The standards movement asserts that all students should understand content at deeper, more complex levels than have been advocated previously for any but the most advanced students. A variety of teaching and learning strategies have been shown to be effective in assisting adolescent learners to develop their capacity as readers and writers. Nevertheless, according to this paper, there is an "ever-deepening crisis in adolescent literacy." The paper considers how effective content-based literacy instruction can be brought to life in the classroom in ways that will make a positive difference for students. It discusses the following questions: Why are educational practitioners and policymakers concerned about adolescent literacy now? What recent developments have taken place on the national and state levels? What would a successful approach to improving adolescent literacy include? What is the Adolescent Literacy Support Framework? How does the framework address the needs of all students? What does adolescent literacy development look like at the classroom level? How will adolescent literacy across the curriculum improve test scores? What do educational leaders need to know?

Meltzer, J., and Okashige, S. E. (2001, October). First literacy, then learning. *Principal Leadership* 2(2), 16–21. (ERIC Document Reproduction Service No. EJ634799).

Discusses four key components of the Adolescent Literacy Support Framework: motivation, implementing research-based literacy strategies, supporting across-the-curriculum reading and writing, and ensuring supportive and sustaining organizational structures and leadership capacity. Describes what the literacy framework might look like if adopted at classroom level in English, mathematics, science, and social studies.

Montgomery, M. (2005, February). Authentic science writing. *Principal Leadership* 5(6), 28–31.

A high school develops reading and writing skills by having students write scientific abstracts about investigations.

Moore, D. W., Bean, T. W., Birdyshaw, D., and Rycik, J. A. (1999). Adolescent literacy: A position statement for the Commission on Adolescent Literacy of the International Reading Association. (ERIC Document Reproduction Service No. ED437640).

Many people do not recognize reading development as a continuum, but the literacy needs of the adolescent reader are far different from those of primary-grade children. This position paper discusses some of those literacy needs and outlines seven principles supporting adolescents' literacy growth. Adolescents deserve (1) access to a wide variety of reading material; (2) instruction that builds both the skill and the desire to read increasingly complex materials; (3) assessment that shows them their strengths as well as their needs and that guides their teachers to design instruction that will best help them grow as readers; (4) expert teachers who model and provide explicit instruction in reading comprehension and study strategies across the curriculum; (5) reading specialists who assist students having difficulty learning to read; (6) teachers who understand the complexities of individual adolescent readers, respect their differences, and respond to their characteristics; and (7) homes, communities, and a nation that will support their efforts to achieve advanced levels of literacy and provide support for them to succeed.

Rycik, J. A., and Irvin, J. L. (2001). *What Adolescents Deserve: A Commitment to Students' Literacy Learning.* (ERIC Document Reproduction Service No. ED450367).

Compiled to help staff developers, administrators, teachers, and policymakers reexamine current literacy practices and reimagine how they can work with each other and with parents and community members, this collection of 22 previously published articles from various professional journals and one new article offers examples of how educators can revitalize their efforts for teaching middle school and high school students and form a better understanding of youth cultures and adolescents' everyday lives. Developed as an extension of the International Reading Association's "Adolescent Literacy: A Position Statement," the volume focuses on four commitments the editors believe are critical to achieving results for adolescent literacy learners: literacy access for all students, challenging and supportive instruction, comprehensive and collaborative programs, and reimagining adolescent literacy learning. After an introduction by the editors, essays in section one, "A Commitment to Literacy Access for All Students," are "Combining Enablement and Engagement to Assist Students Who Do Not Read and Write Well" (Mary F. Roe); "An Effective (and Affordable) Intervention Model for At-Risk High School Readers" (Cynthia Fischer); "Against Marginalization and Criminal Reading Curriculum Standards for African American Adolescents in Low-Level Tracks: A Retrospective of Baldwin's Essay" (Alfred W. Tatum); "What Middle and High School Educators Need to Know About Language Minority Students" (Elizabeth G. Sturtevant); and "A Library for Ophelia" (Marsha M. Sprague and Kara K. Keeling). Essays in section two, "A Commitment to Challenging and Supportive Instruction," are "Discovering Readers in the Middle Level School: A Few Helpful Clues" (Gay Ivey); "Motivating Secondary School Students to Read Their Textbooks" (Barbara L. McCombs and Mary Lee Barton); "One Teacher's Use of Computers and Technology: A Look Inside a Classroom" (Mary Santerre); "Writing Portfolios: Active vs. Passive" (Bonita L. Wilcox); and "Is This Really English?: Using Young Adult Literature in an Urban

Middle School" (Rebecca J. Joseph). Essays in section three, "A Commitment to Comprehensive and Collaborative Programs," are "Exemplary Literacy Learning Programs" (Susan E. Strauss and Judith L. Irvin); "Supporting the Development of Strong Middle Grades Readers" (Jack W. Humphrey); "Creating a Middle School Culture of Literacy" (Robert Feirsen); "The Literacy Council: People Are the Key to an Effective Program" (Patricia L. Anders); "A New Role for the Reading Specialist: Contributing Toward a High School's Collaborative Educational Culture" (Geraldine F. Henwood); "From Information to Interaction: Involving Parents in the Literacy Development of Their Adolescent" (James A. Rycik); "Reaching Beyond Yourself: A Middle School Service Learning Program" (Martha A. Magner); and "Using Data to Improve Literacy Learning for High School Students" (Michael C. Biance and Judith L. Irvin). Essays in section four, "A Commitment to Reimagining Adolescent Literacy Learning," are "Reflections on the Past, Directions for the Future" (Harold M. Foster); "Developing Critical and Imaginative Thinking Within Electronic Literacy" (Marino C. Alvarez); "Rock 'n' Roll and Horror Stories: Students, Teachers, and Popular Culture" (Cynthia Lewis); "Intergenerational Conversations and Two Adolescents' Multiple Literacies: Implications for Redefining Content Area Literacy" (Thomas W. Bean, Shannon K. Bean, and Kristen F. Bean); and "Beginning to Create the New Literacy Classroom: What Does the New Literacy Look Like?" (William Kist).

Stevens, L. P. (2002, Spring). Making the road by walking: The transition from content area literacy to adolescent literacy. *Reading Research and Instruction* 41(3), 267–78. (ERIC Document Reproduction Service No. EJ646975).

Explores complexities of plotting the transition from the term "content-area reading" to "adolescent literacy" through the content of a preservice content-area literacy class. Uses students' online discussions as data. Compares results to work in adolescent literacy in Australia. Suggests examination of potential barriers and benefits of reconceptualizing the content, format, and placement of courses on content-area literacy.

Strong, Julia. (2001). *Literacy across the Curriculum: Making It Happen.* London: Collins Educational.

This photocopiable pack provides guidance and support for literacy coordinators in each subject area, helping them to apply and deliver the whole-school literacy development policy in each curriculum area. Supports and applies the Language for Learning initiative in a practical, classroom-focused manner; gives practical examples of literacy-focused activities that can be used across the curriculum. All materials have been developed with and tested by classroom teachers in each faculty area. Written by Julia Strong, an experienced former class teacher and now deputy director of the Literacy Trust.

Strong, Julia. (1999). *Literacy at 11–14: A Practical Guide to Raising Achievement through Whole-School Literacy.* London: Collins Educational.

Literacy at 11–14 is a photocopiable guide to developing a literacy strategy suitable for Key Stage 3. It contains practical guidance and ready-to-run activities, and focuses on developing literacy across the curriculum. 1. Introducing literacy to your school; 2. Language across the curriculum: involving all subject areas; 3. Developing your whole-school approach to literacy; 4. Running a literacy INSET day in your school.

Urquhart, V. (2005, February). Improving writing: What principals can do. *Principal Leadership* 5(6), 44–48.

Principals should promote instructional methods that improve writing skills and encourage teachers to use writing in every content area.

Vacca, R. T. (2002, November). From efficient decoders to strategic readers. *Educational Leadership* 60(3), 6–11. (ERIC Document Reproduction Service No. EJ655406).

Describes the use of content-area reading and writing programs to address the problems of adolescent literacy. Provides examples of how content-area teachers incorporate reading and writing instruction strategies in their classes.

Zipperer, F. M. J., Worley, M. T., Sisson, M. W., and Said, R. W. (2002, September). Literacy education and reading programs in the secondary school: Status, problems, and solutions. *NASSP Bulletin* 86(632), 3–17.

The status of literacy education and the reading program at the secondary school level is examined. Current problems and possible solutions for those problems are discussed. Results of a survey of principals' perceptions of their reading programs in a local school system are analyzed and supported by appropriate literature on the topic.

Reading Strategies for Adolescent Literacy in High School

Agnew, M. L. (2000, March). DRAW: A motivational reading comprehension strategy for disaffected readers. *Journal of Adolescent & Adult Literacy* 43(6), 574–576. (ERIC Document Reproductive Service No. EJ601071).

Describes a strategy adaptable for middle school, high school, and college levels that helps to motivate students to want to read and gain information; promotes discussion and fosters students' learning from one another; helps below-grade-level readers understand content; and encourages higher-order thinking.

Allen, J. (2001, October). Eliminating a "yes, but" curriculum. *Principal Leadership* 2(2), 10–15. (ERIC Document Reproductive Service No. EJ634798).

Identifies several impediments to achieving reading literacy for many in-city high school students in California, including lack of interest and motivation, inappropriate resources, absence of support, and insufficient reading experiences and background knowledge. Recommends ways to remove these barriers through the use of strategic reading and supporting and celebrating success.

Alvermann, D. E., and Strickland, D. S. (2004). *Bridging the Literacy Achievement Gap: Grades 4–12.* New York, NY: Teachers College Press.

This book addresses critical issues related to preadolescent and adolescent literacy learners with a focus on closing the achievement gap. Despite efforts by educators and policymakers during the past several decades, certain groups of students— primarily African American students, English language learners, and students from low-income homes—continue to underperform on commonly used measures of academic achievement. Too often, teachers and administrators lack both proper preparation and good ideas to confront these issues. Part I of this volume contains essential background information about specific populations of learners who are not achieving as well as expected. Part II provides descriptions of promising programs that are authored and co-authored by practitioners and researchers working collaboratively. The result is a valuable resource for those involved in teaching and setting policy for literacy education in grades 4–12.

Barton, M. L. (1997, March). Addressing the literacy crisis: Teaching reading in the content areas. *NASSP Bulletin* 81(587), 22–30. (ERIC Document Reproductive Service No. EJ540820).

Middle-level and high school teachers must be skilled in content-area reading strategies and be able to teach their students strategic informational reading skills. Students who learn how to skillfully use background knowledge, text-feature knowledge (headings, graphics, and vocabulary), and metacognitive knowledge will become strategic readers. Since students must learn to read in all content areas, every teacher must be a reading teacher.

Biancarosa, G., and Snow, C. (2004). *Reading Next: A Vision for Action and Research in Middle and High School Literacy.* A report to Carnegie Corporation of New York. Washington, DC: Alliance for Excellent Education.

This report combines the best research currently available with well-crafted strategies for turning that research into practice. Written by five of the nation's leading researchers, *Reading Next* charts an immediate route to improving adolescent literacy. The authors outline 15 key elements of an effective literacy intervention and call on public and private stakeholders to invest in the literacy of middle and high school students today, while simultaneously building the knowledge base.

Brozo, W. G., and Hargis, C. H. (2003, September). Taking seriously the idea of reform: One high school's efforts to make reading more responsive to all students. *Journal of Adolescent & Adult Literacy* 47(1), 14–23. (ERIC Document Reproductive Service No. EJ676043).

Describes how subject-area teachers at one high school used grant money to change their teaching styles, significantly improving students' reading abilities. Details how reading achievement testing was conducted and the results were translated into effective literacy reforms designed to go beyond "teaching to the middle." Tracks the experiences of two students at either end of the reading ability continuum and the effects the initiatives had on them.

Codding, J. (2001, October). An up ramp for struggling readers. *Principal Leadership* 2(2), 22–25. (ERIC Document Reproductive Service No. EJ634800).

Describes a year-long high school reading and writing literacy course developed by the National Center on Education and the Economy, designed to be delivered in a 90-minute, double-block period, five days a week. Identifies several things principals can do to successfully implement the course.

Fisher, D., Frey, N., and Williams, D. (2002, November). Seven literacy strategies that work. *Educational Leadership* 60(3), 70–73. (ERIC Document Reproductive Service No. EJ655420).

Describes seven instructional strategies to improve student reading and writing across the curriculum at Herbert Hoover High School in San Diego, California. Strategies include read-alouds, "K-W-L charts," graphic organizers, vocabulary instruction, writing to learn, structured note-taking, and reciprocal teaching.

Forget, M., Lyle, N., Spear, M., and Reinhart-Clark, K. (2003). Getting all teachers to use reading/writing to help students learn subject matter. Paper presented at the annual meeting of the International Reading Association, Orlando, FL. (ERIC Document Reproductive Service No. ED479376).

Generally speaking, reading is not taught beyond the third grade in most school systems. If a student has not mastered reading comprehension skills by the fourth grade, chances are that he or she will struggle with learning in grades 4 through 12. Many middle school and high school students lack the ability to use communication skills effectively for the purpose of learning. This paper discusses "MAX" (Motivation, Acquisition, and eXtension) teaching with reading and writing: a rationale and a method. Before discussing MAX teaching, the paper presents an "anticipation guide," a worksheet that quizzes teachers on how students learn most effectively. It then discusses "embedded curriculum," in which learning skills are taught in conjunction with course content. The paper states that the essential goal of teachers who use the MAX teaching framework is to level the playing field by raising the bar for all students, which involves creating a classroom environment that provides instruction in building skills to enable improved performance, while at the same time engaging all students in active learning from textbooks and other forms of textual matter. It explains each of the steps of MAX teaching and considers how frequently teachers should use MAX. The paper concludes by outlining how to prepare teachers to use MAX.

Kamil, M. L. (2003). *Adolescents and Literacy: Reading for the 21st Century.* Washington, DC: Alliance for Excellent Education.

This report examines the reliable, empirical research that exists on how to improve the literacy of children in grades 4 through 12. It brings together the key findings of the best available research on issues related to adolescent literacy. It also offers policymakers and the public a better understanding of the challenges and opportunities that confront the nation as it begins to work to improve the literacy levels of older children. The report demonstrates that we already know a great deal about reading comprehension and about effective methods for helping students of all ages become better readers.

Kemp, C. (2005, February). A comprehensive approach to adolescent literacy. *Principal Leadership* 5(6), 22–27.

A district's comprehensive literacy strategy includes assigning literacy coaches to all high schools, providing professional training for all staff members, and using educational technology to promote literacy.

Lash, R. (2005, February). Building reading skills step by step. *Principal Leadership* 5(6), 38–42.

FAME, a reading program that builds upon the strengths of students and involves parents, allows students who are reading below grade level to make roughly a one-year grade-equivalent gain for each semester of instruction.

Laverick, C. (2002, October). B-D-A strategy: Reinventing the wheel can be a good thing. *Journal of Adolescent & Adult Literacy* 46(2), 144–47. (ERIC Document Reproductive Service No. EJ653526).

Presents a remodeled reading strategy for high school students that is based on K-W-L and some of its variations. Develops a strategy handout that both teachers and students could use and that would facilitate teaching the curriculum rather than taking time away from it. Notes that the "B-D-A" labels the essential before, during, and after steps.

Metzger, M. (1998, November). Teaching reading: Beyond the plot. *Phi Delta Kappan* 80(3), 240–46. (ERIC Document Reproductive Service No. EJ575215).

To help reluctant high school readers, a ninth-grade teacher modified a pedagogy called the Socratic Seminar (the Paedeia Approach) based on the work of Mortimer Adler and Dennis Gray. A Socratic Seminar is a focused discussion on a short piece of writing. The process is explained.

Riggs, E. G., and Gil-Garcia, A. (2001). *Helping Middle and High School Readers: Teaching and Learning Strategies across the Curriculum.* ERS What We Know About series. Arlington, VA: Educational Research Service. (ERIC Document Reproduction Service No. ED458550).

Although middle and high school teachers rightfully view the teaching of subject-area content as their primary responsibility, there is an increasing recognition that they must also play an active role in ensuring that students are not left behind because of reading problems. This report emphasizes that middle and high school teachers do not need to be reading specialists and do not need to take time away from essential content-area instruction to help their students become more proficient in this critical skill. The contention is that they can, however, integrate the teaching and learning strategies described in the report into their content-area instruction on a daily basis. The report is based on research findings, informed opinions from the professional literature, and a wealth of examples from educators' experience. It is divided into the following sections: Introduction; Understanding the Problem: How Poor Learning Strategies Limit Students' Reading Success; Building Strong, Strategic Readers; Learning Strategy 1: Metacognition; Learning Strategy 2: Prior Knowledge; Learning Strategy 3: Inferencing; Learning Strategy 4: Text Structure; Learning Strategy 5: Vocabulary Development and Acquisition; The Next Step: Educating and Supporting Teachers; and Pulling It All Together: Taking a Schoolwide Approach to Instruction in Reading Strategies.

Rose, A. (2000, November–December). Literacy strategies at the secondary level. *Leadership* 30(2), 12–16. (ERIC Document Reproductive Service No. EJ617869).

Many high school students responding to a teacher's in-class literacy survey are frustrated, unprepared readers, lacking metacognitive knowledge and comprehension monitoring. Respondents own few books, avoid libraries, and cannot name a favorite book title. They must be taught to question, predict, summarize, and clarify until meanings emerge.

Schoenbach, C. G., Cziko, C., and Hurwitz, L. (1999). *Reading for Understanding: A Guide to Improving Reading in Middle and High School Classrooms.* San Francisco, CA: Jossey-Bass. (ERIC Document Reproduction Service No. ED437618).

Many middle school and high school students have difficulty reading and understanding academic texts, which limits their ability to meet today's high learning standards. This guidebook addresses this quiet but growing crisis. Aimed at content-area teachers in secondary schools, the guidebook describes a successful approach to helping students improve their literacy across all subject areas. The guidebook describes a program in which an entire freshman class in one urban high school increased its average reading scores by more than two years. Piloted in San Francisco, the groundbreaking Academic Literacy program proved that it was not too late for teachers and students to work together in boosting literacy, engagement, and achievement. Easy to read and filled with classroom lessons and exercises, the guidebook shows teachers how they can create classroom "reading apprenticeships" to help students build reading comprehension skills and relate what they read to a larger knowledge base. It also discusses the strategies and support systems needed to implement and evaluate reading apprenticeship programs throughout a school. The guidebook can be a companion for educators ready to face the challenge of building reading into their content-area teaching. Appendixes contain a curriculum overview of the first unit taught in the Academic Literacy course and a discussion of evaluation instruments used.

Sharp, P., and Ashby, D. (2002). *Improving Student Comprehension Skills through Instructional Strategies.* Unpublished dissertation. (ERIC Document Reproductive Service No. ED468240).

This report describes a program designed to enhance reading comprehension. Reading comprehension relies on skills that enable students to remember facts, draw out main ideas, make inferences, and relate reading to personal experiences. The focus group consisted of middle and high school students in a metropolitan area in northern Illinois. Analysis of probable cause data indicated that students had a lack of motivation and fluency in reading, limited vocabulary, limited background knowledge, and a minimal interest in material being read. The literature has indicated that intrinsic motivation for literacy declines in middle school. For students to be part of today's ever-changing society and workforce, reading comprehension is an essential skill. A review of solution strategies suggested by researchers has resulted in possible solutions through interventions. The various instructional methods include thinking-skill instruction, cooperative groups, multiple intelligence strategies, and metacognition skills. Postintervention data indicated an increase in students' reading comprehension skills. Appendixes contain a sample of Rhody Secondary Reading Attitude Assessment, a sample of Reading Interest Inventory, and a sample of Gates-MacGinitie reading tests.

Spor, M. (2005, February). Reading to learn. *Principal Leadership* 5(6), 16–21.

Reading strategies that involve students before, during, and after reading are effective and increase students' retention and comprehension.

Sturtevant, E. G. (2003). *The Literacy Coach: A Key to Improving Teaching and Learning in Secondary Schools.* Washington, DC: Alliance for Excellent Education.

Helps to develop an understanding of what works in successful programs as well as successful strategies for training effective literacy coaches.

Taylor, R., Hasselbring, T. S., and Williams, R. D. (2001, October). Reading, writing, and misbehavior. *Principal Leadership* 2(2), 33–38. (ERIC Document Reproductive Service No. EJ634802).

Asserts that student misbehavior is linked to poor reading and writing skills. Suggests ways to improve reading and writing literacy based on experience with a literacy program in the Orange County (FL) public schools. Three-year study of the program found significant improvement in reading comprehension, student self-esteem, and classroom behavior.

Taylor, R. T., Jones, P., and Mills, J. (2005, February). Fail-safe literacy. *Principal Leadership* 5(6), 28–31.

By having teachers learn literacy strategies and tailoring instruction to students' skill levels, a high school significantly improves student literacy.

Taylor, S. V., and Nesheim, D. W. (2001, October). Creating meaning in a readers' workshop. *Principal Leadership* 2(2), 47–49. (ERIC Document Reproductive Service No. EJ634805).

Describes the content and organization of a readers' workshop, an approach to reading instruction for high school students with poor reading skills that emphasizes the building of connections between students' life experiences and providing a structured, shared reading-learning environment. Identifies resources for selecting children's literature.

Weller, L. D., and Weller, S. J. (1997, May). Using Deming's continuous improvement model to improve reading. *NASSP Bulletin* 81(589), 78–85. (ERIC Document Reproductive Service No. EJ544322).

To improve student's reading scores on the Test of Achievement and Proficiency, a rural Georgia high school initiated an improvement program based on Deming's continuous-improvement model in fall 1995. This model allows those closest to the problem to resolve it. By working continuously to improve students' testing environment, test-taking knowledge, and reading comprehension, the plan spurred a significant rise in spring 1996 reading scores.

Wilhelm, J. D., Baker, T. N., and Dube, J. (2001). *Strategic Reading: Guiding Students to Lifelong Literacy, 6–12.* Westport, CT: Heinemann. (ERIC Document Reproductive Service No. ED455490).

As students move on to more challenging texts in middle and high school, their reading skills do not grow automatically to meet those demands. They need help figuring out "how" to read, not just "what" to read. As the focus on reading more sophisticated kinds of texts intensifies in schools, students need more help than ever. This book provides the tools teachers need to help students of all abilities make this important transition to higher-level texts. The book relies on a "learning-centered" approach to reading. It offers a thorough examination of the issues surrounding teaching and learning, and of the specific demands particular texts make on readers. Then it provides many innovative strategies for teaching students to comprehend, engage, and make use of these kinds of texts. Following an introduction, the book is divided into these chapters: (1) A Theory of Teaching; (2) A Theory of Teaching Reading; (3) Authorial Reading and Democratic Projects; (4) Frontloading: Teaching before Reading; (5) Loving the Questions: Fostering Student Questioning and Discussion; (6) Building on Different Strengths to Make Reading Visible; (7) Assignment Sequencing: Teaching Students Text by Text, Activity by Activity; and (8) Reading Together.

Wilson, E. A. (1999). *Reading at the Middle and High School Levels: Building Active Readers across the Curriculum.* 2nd ed. ERS What We Know About series. Arlington, VA: Educational Research Service. (ERIC Document Reproduction Service No. ED388955).

Based on research findings, informed opinions contained in the professional literature, and examples from school personnel of "what works," this report focuses on strategies that educators can use to improve secondary school students' reading skills and enhance interest in reading. Many of the strategies in the report are applicable across the curriculum—not just in English classes, but also in subjects such as science and social studies. Sections of the report are (1) Introduction: Issues Surrounding Secondary School Reading, (2) Motivational Factors Related to Reading, (3) Approaches for Actively Engaging Students in Reading, (4) Metacognition: Developing Good Reading Strategies, (5) Other Techniques to Improve Reading Skills, (6) Assessment: Purposes and Approaches, (7) Issues Specific to Content Area Reading Instruction, and (8) Concluding Remarks.

Vacca, R. T. (2002, November). From efficient decoders to strategic readers. *Educational Leadership* 60(3), 6–11. (ERIC Document Reproductive Service No. EJ655406).

Describes the use of content reading and writing programs to address the problems of adolescent literacy. Provides examples of how content-area teachers incorporate reading and writing instruction strategies in their classes.

Appendix 2:
Literacy Capacity Survey

Directions:

Step 1: Please rate your own perceived degree of importance for each item below on a scale of 1 to 5 in the first column to the right, *Important to Our School's Literacy Initiative.*

Step 2: Please rate the degree to which each activity is currently in practice at your school on a scale of 1 to 5 in the second column to the right, *Current Practice at Our School.*

Step 3: When you have rated all items in both columns, please return this completed survey for compilation with those completed by other staff members at your school.

Importance rating: 5 = Very Important 1 = Not Important **Practice Rating:** 5 = Frequent or common practice at this school. 1 = An infrequent or rare occurrence at this school.	Important to Our School's Literacy Initiative	Current Practice at Our School
Collaborative Leadership and School Capacity		
1. The administrator's role in improving the school's literacy opportunities is clearly evident.		
2. School leaders encourage collegial decisionmaking.		
3. School leaders support integration of literacy instruction across the content areas.		
4. School leaders and staff members believe the teaching of reading is their responsibility.		
5. Adequate fiscal resources are provided to support the literacy improvement plan.		
6. Data-driven decisionmaking guides literacy improvement planning.		
7. Scheduling structures are in place to support identified literacy needs of all students.		
8. Scheduling structures are in place to support literacy professional development.		
9. The school improvement plan includes literacy as a major goal for improvement.		
Strategic Use of Assessment		
10. A variety of school and student data sources is used to support the instructional improvement focus.		
11. Professional development to improve literacy is based on assessment data.		
12. Standardized, formal assessments are used to assess reading ability of all students.		
13. Teachers know the reading capabilities of all students they teach.		
14. Data meetings guide formative and summative literacy planning to support student learning.		
15. Ongoing progress monitoring identifies skills mastered and skills that continue to be focus of student's intervention plan.		
16. Teachers use informal reading assessments within content classes to develop a better understanding of student literacy instructional needs.		

Professional Development to Support Literacy		
17. The Literacy Leadership Team assesses and plans literacy professional development focus.		
18. Professional development plans are based on identified student literacy needs.		
19. Reflective teaching and self-assessment of instructional practices provide direction as to ongoing literacy professional planning.		
20. Content-area teachers receive professional development to learn literacy strategies.		
21. Teachers with literacy expertise and experience serve as models and mentors to less experienced colleagues.		
22. Data from informal *Literacy Walks* provide areas of focus for literacy professional development.		
23. Teachers participate in shared-teaching sessions to learn and refine literacy strategies.		
24. Content area teachers receive ongoing, job-embedded professional development to learn instructional/literacy strategies.		
Instructional Practices		
25. Teachers use effective instructional practices in support of developing student literacy and comprehensions of course content.		
26. Teachers effectively use a variety of before, during, and after reading strategies to support learning and literacy.		
27. Teachers provide personalized support to each student to improve literacy based on assessed needs.		
28. Teachers create literacy-rich environments with books, journals, and research texts to support content learning.		
29. Teachers effectively use small group instructional strategies to improve student learning and comprehension of course content.		
30. Teachers effectively model how to use a variety of literacy/learning strategies for all students.		
31. Teachers effectively use a variety of literacy strategies that support learning of specific content texts for all students.		
32. Teachers use technology to support improved literacy for all students.		
33. Teachers regularly use vocabulary development strategies to support student learning.		
34. Teachers regularly use strategies to support the reading/writing connection.		
Intervention to Improve Student Achievement		
35. Administrators and teachers develop individual literacy plans to meet literacy instructional needs of struggling students.		
36. Intervention is highly prescriptive toward improving identified literacy deficits of individuals.		
37. Literacy electives are available to support improved literacy of struggling students and English language learners.		
38. Ample tutoring sessions are available to support improved student literacy.		
39. The most highly skilled teachers work with struggling/striving readers.		
40. Content teachers effectively use literacy strategies to support struggling/striving readers' learning of content texts.		
41. The School Literacy Improvement Plan supports strategies ranging from intervention for struggling readers to expanding the reading power of all students.		

Appendix 3:
Literacy Team Planning Guide

If secondary schools are to meet the academic instructional needs of each student, there are several key elements that must be in place. These essentials include (a) supportive and actively involved school leaders, (b) formal and informal assessments that guide the learning of students and teachers, (c) a research-based professional development program, (d) a comprehensive plan for strategic and accelerated intervention, and (e) highly skilled teachers in every content area that model and provide explicit instruction to improve comprehension. Although the task can appear to be overwhelming at first, a collaborative effort of administrators, faculty, and other key individuals can achieve a successful adolescent literacy program that will lead to student success.

Literacy Leadership Team: Questions to Consider

Begin the journey to literacy improvement by discussing the following questions:

1. How has your leadership supported literacy efforts at your school? Do *all* your teachers view literacy as an integral part of the academic program? What structures and resources have you put in place to encourage literacy for all?

2. What do your assessment scores reveal about your school's literacy practices? How is data being used to guide your school improvement plan? Do teachers have access to the data and use it to guide their instructional practices?

3. What do you consider the key elements of your school's professional development plan? How do data and student literacy needs guide the development of the plan? Does your school structure support professional development by allowing time for professional conversations, for examining student work, and for learning new literacy strategies?

4. Are your content-area teachers skilled at integrating literacy strategies into their daily lessons? What training have you provided for your teachers so they can be highly effective at delivering instruction in reading in their content areas? Are your struggling students being taught by your most effective teachers?

5. What support does your school provide for students who are below grade level in reading? Does your schedule provide these students with additional, not pull-out, time to improve their skills? Do your teachers use instructional strategies that support struggling students as they read textbooks and other content-area material?

Planning Tool

Area of Focus	Guiding Questions	Action Required
Leadership and School Structure		
	1. How will the Literacy Leadership Team (LLT) encourage staff support of a schoolwide literacy initiative?	
	2. Will schedule changes be required to support additional time for reading, intervention, and professional development?	
	3. How will the literacy focus become a major component of the school improvement plan?	
	4. What steps/activities will the LLT need to develop to ensure collaborative conversations and planning?	
Strategic Use of Assessment		
	1. Identify formal reading assessments to be used to identify specific reading weaknesses.	
	2. Identify informal assessments to be used for ongoing monitoring of student progress.	
	3. How will school data be analyzed to identify professional development needs of staff?	
	4. How will struggling/striving readers be identified?	
	5. How will the LLT share student literacy data with the staff?	
	6. How often will data meetings be conducted during the year?	
	7. How often will the Teams meet to monitor progress of struggling/striving readers?	
Professional Development		
	1. What initial professional development will be planned?	
	2. How will ongoing assessments of student progress identify additional professional development needs?	
	3. How will on-going professional development requirements be identified to improve literacy instructional strategies?	
	4. How will collaborative teaching opportunities such as shared teaching and peer coaching to support literacy instruction be integrated into plan?	
	5. What actions are necessary to create a culture of reflective teaching and self-assessment to support literacy?	
Instructional Practices		
	1. Identify strategies to support effective integration of pre, during, and post reading strategies across the content area classrooms.	
	2. How will teachers effectively support the reading/writing connection?	
	3. Identify supports to effectively integrate technology into literacy instruction.	
	4. How will literacy-rich environments be created within each classroom?	
	5. How will teachers effectively assist students with learning content vocabulary?	
	6. How will effective use of small group instructional strategies be supported?	
	7. How will teachers identify and use literacy strategies to support learning of content?	

Area of Focus	Guiding Questions	Action Required
Intervention Strategies		
	1. How will identified individual literacy needs of struggling students be met? Additional class?	
	2. How will specific prescriptive literacy strategies become a vital ingredient of the Individual Literacy Improvement Plan?	
	3. How will content teachers support literacy needs of struggling students within daily instructional strategies?	
	4. Will additional tutoring options be available to support students?	
	5. What additional technology support may be needed to support literacy learning?	
	6. What monitoring structures are required to identify student progress and achievement of benchmarks?	
	7. What schoolwide strategies are in place to expand the reading power of ALL students—struggling to gifted?	

Appendix 4:
Literacy Improvement
Action Plan Template

Goal					
Objective	Action Steps	Persons Responsible	Timeline	Resources	Evaluation

Appendix 5:
Assessments for Middle and High School Students

Assessment	Assesses	Group or Individual Administration/Time	Publisher
Developmental Reading Assessment (Grades 4–8)	Fluency and comprehension	Individual, 5–7 minutes	Pearson Learning, 2002
Comprehensive Test of Phonological Processing (CTOPP) (Grades K–16)	Phonological awareness, phonological memory, and rapid naming	Individual, 30 minutes	AGS Publishing, 1999 PRO-ED, 1999 Wagner, Torgeson, Rasholte
Test of Reading Comprehension (TORC-3) (Ages 7–17)	Comprehension, vocabulary, syntactic similarities, paragraph reading, sentence sequencing. Measures content area vocabulary in Math, Social Studies, and Science.	Individual/Group, 30 minutes	AGS Publishing, 1995 PRO-ED, 1995 Brown, Hammill, Wiederholt
Group Reading Assessment and Diagnostic Evaluation (GRADE) (Ages: 5–Adult)	Comprehension, vocabulary, English skills	Group, 60–90 minutes	AGS Publishing, 2000 Williams, Cassidy, Samuels
Scholastic Reading Inventory (Ages 6–17)	Vocabulary, fluency, passage details, cause and effect relationships, sequencing, drawing conclusions, making connections, and generalizations	Computerized individual assessment	Scholastic
Test of Word Reading Efficiency (TOWRE) (Ages 6–24)	Measures the ability to accurately recognize familiar words as whole units or sight words and the ability to sound out words quickly	Individual, 5–10 minutes	PRO-ED, 1999
Degrees of Reading Power (DRP) (Grades 1–12)	Measures reading comprehension using nonfiction and prose paragraphs that are similar to CLOZE Procedure	Individual/Group, Untimed	Touchstone Applied Science Associations, Inc. (TASA)

Assessment	Assesses	Group or Individual Administration/Time	Publisher
Burns/Roe Informal Reading Inventory (Ages 5–18)	Comprehension, retellings, graded word lists for placement with graded reading selections	Individual	Riverside, 1999 Roe
Reading Inventory for the Classroom, 4th Ed. (Grades K–12)	Reading of connected text, word analysis, comprehension, miscue analysis, listening comprehension	Individual	Prentice Hall, 2001
Gray Oral Reading Test-Diagnostic (GORT-D) (Ages 5–12)	Paragraph reading, decoding, word identification, word attack, morphemic analysis, contextual analysis, and word ordering	Individual	PRO-ED, 1991
Gray Silent Reading Test (Ages 7–25)	Measures silent reading and comprehension	Individual	PRO-ED, 2000
Qualitative Reading Inventory-3rd Ed. (QRI-III), (Ages 6–13)	Assesses oral reading accuracy, rate, strategies, comprehension, word identification	Individual	Allyn and Bacon, 2000
Gates-MacGinitie Reading Test, 4th Ed. (Grades K–12)	General assessment of reading achievement, vocabulary/word knowledge, comprehension	Individual or group, 55–105 minutes	Riverside, 1998
Woodcock Reading Mastery, revised (Grades K–12)	Evaluates visual auditory learning, letter identification, word identification, word comprehension, and passage comprehension	Individual, 90 minutes	AGS Publishing, 1998
Stanford Diagnostic Reading Test – 4th Ed. (SDRT-4) (Grades 1–12)	Identifies specific strengths and weaknesses in phonetic analysis, vocabulary, comprehension, and scanning	Group, 90 minutes	Harcourt, Inc.
Analytical Reading Inventory, 6th Ed., (Grades K–12)	Contains narrative and expository passages designed to assess level of instruction, strategies to recognize words and comprehend books, oral and silent reading performance	Individual	Prentice Hall Woods, Moe

Appendix 6:
Five-Year Data Collecting Template

	Year 1:	Year 2:	Year 3:	Year 4:	Year 5:
Standardized Tests:					
Reading					
Language Arts					
Math					
Social Studies					
Graduation Exam:					
English					
Math					
Science					
Social Studies					
Writing Assessments					
End of Course Tests:					
Math					
History					
English					
Science					
Advanced Placement Tests:					
Math					
History					
English					
Science					
SAT					
ACT					

Appendix 7:
Progress Monitoring Template

Name: _____ Grade: _____ Date: _____

Grades	Math	English	History	Science
GP$_1$				
GP$_2$				
GP$_3$				
GP$_4$				

GP = Grading Period

Formal Reading Assessment

Test Used:

Pre Assessment	Post Assessment
Date:	Date:
Standard Score _____	Standard Score _____
Comprehension _____	Comprehension _____
Vocabulary _____	Vocabulary _____

Informal Reading Assessment

1st Grading Period	2nd Grading Period
Comprehension:	**Comprehension:**
___Main Idea ___Recall ___Cause/Effect ___Comparison ___Predictions ___Context Clues ___Follow Directions ___Conclusions	___Main Idea ___Recall ___Cause/Effect ___Comparison ___Predictions ___Context Clues ___Follow Directions ___Conclusions
Word Identification:	**Word Identification:**
___ # of words missed ___ # miscues/substitutions ___ timed reading responses	___ # of words missed ___ # miscues/substitutions ___ timed reading responses
3rd Grading Period	**4th Grading Period**
Comprehension:	**Comprehension:**
___Main Idea ___Recall ___Cause/Effect ___Comparison ___Predictions ___Context Clues ___Follow Directions ___Conclusions	___Main Idea ___Recall ___Cause/Effect ___Comparison ___Predictions ___Context Clues ___Follow Directions ___Conclusions
Word Identification:	**Word Identification:**
___ # of words missed ___ # miscues/substitutions ___ timed reading responses	___ # of words missed ___ # miscues/substitutions ___ timed reading responses

Other Information:

Recommended Instructional Strategies:

GP$_1$	
GP$_2$	
GP$_3$	
GP$_4$	

Appendix B
Braingame.joystick Enquiries

Appendix 8:
Disaggregated Data Template

	Quartile 1								Quartile 2								Quartile 3								Quartile 4							
Year/Grade	W	B	H	AI	PI	F/R	ELL		W	B	H	AI	PI	F/R	ELL		W	B	H	AI	PI	F/R	ELL		W	B	H	AI	PI	F/R	ELL	
Year:																																
Grade ____																																
Grade ____																																
Grade ____																																
Grade ____																																
Year:																																
Grade ____																																
Grade ____																																
Grade ____																																
Grade ____																																
Year:																																
Grade ____																																
Grade ____																																
Grade ____																																
Grade ____																																
Year:																																
Grade ____																																
Grade ____																																
Grade ____																																
Grade ____																																
Year:																																
Grade ____																																
Grade ____																																
Grade ____																																
Grade ____																																

W = White
B = Black
H = Hispanic
AI = American Indian
PI = Pacific Islander
F/R = Free/Reduced Lunch
ELL = English Language Learner

Index

C

D

E

F

G

H

I

L

M

N

P

T

Teacher guidelines, 31–32

Teacher networks, 39

Teachers, 2–3, 4, 45, 46. *See also* Professional development
  action steps for highly effective, 47–50
  attitudes and perceptions, 67
  collegial atmosphere for, 31, 39
  content-area, 1, 4, 10, 11, 31, 45, 62–63
  determining learning needs of, 32
  encouraging, 28–29, 33, 47
  focused literacy conversation/discussion, 34–35
  goalsetting for, 47
  grouping students for learning, 39
  hiring, 47
  mentor teaching/coaching opportunities, 34, 54–55
  multiple approaches to teaching, 39
  multiple-level staff communication, 29
  peer teaching/coaching, 29, 33–34, 39
  points to remember, 50
  preparing, 21
  quality sharing among, 33
  research and expert opinions on, 50–52
  self-evaluation, 40
  for struggling students, 59

Testing companies, collaboration with, 23

Textbook aides, using, 51

Title funds, 12

Title I teachers, 42

Tutorials, after-school, 28, 55

U

University professor/graduate student assistance, 24

V

Vocabulary and comprehension strategies, 51, 57–58, 63–64

Vocational specialization schools, 41–43

Volunteers, in intervention programs, 60

W

Wallace Foundation, 13

Whole language and phonics instruction, 57, 59, 64

Woodcock Reading Mastery, 66

Writing. *See* Reading and writing

Z

Zoom transition program, 17